CAMBRIDGE LIBRARY COLLECTION

Books of enduring scholarly value

Women's Writing

The later twentieth century saw a huge wave of academic interest in women's writing, which led to the rediscovery of neglected works from a wide range of genres, periods and languages. Many books that were immensely popular and influential in their own day are now studied again, both for their own sake and for what they reveal about the social, political and cultural conditions of their time. A pioneering resource in this area is Orlando: Women's Writing in the British Isles from the Beginnings to the Present (http://orlando.cambridge.org), which provides entries on authors' lives and writing careers, contextual material, timelines, sets of internal links, and bibliographies. Its editors have made a major contribution to the selection of the works reissued in this series within the Cambridge Library Collection, which focuses on non-fiction publications by women on a wide range of subjects from astronomy to biography, music to political economy, and education to prison reform.

Poets and Dreamers

Lady (Augusta) Gregory (1852–1932) was a dramatist and folklorist. Along with the poet W. B. Yeats she was a driving force behind the Irish Literary Revival, and co-founded the Abbey Theatre, Dublin. Born Isabella Augusta Persse in County Galway, she belonged to the Anglo-Irish ascendancy, which was closely associated with colonial rule. She married Sir William Gregory, who was 35 years her senior, in 1880. Her conversion to Irish cultural nationalism began after the death of her husband and was heavily influenced by her visit in 1892 to Inisheer, one of the Aran Islands, where she learnt Irish and the Hiberno-English dialect of Kiltartan. *Poets and Dreamers* was her first publication and contained translations of the Irish-language poet Anthony Raftery, folk-tales, and plays by the Gaelic scholar and future first President of Ireland, Douglas Hyde. For more information on this author, see http://orlando.cambridge.org/public/svPeople?person_id=gregau

Cambridge University Press has long been a pioneer in the reissuing of out-of-print titles from its own backlist, producing digital reprints of books that are still sought after by scholars and students but could not be reprinted economically using traditional technology. The Cambridge Library Collection extends this activity to a wider range of books which are still of importance to researchers and professionals, either for the source material they contain, or as landmarks in the history of their academic discipline.

Drawing from the world-renowned collections in the Cambridge University Library, and guided by the advice of experts in each subject area, Cambridge University Press is using state-of-the-art scanning machines in its own Printing House to capture the content of each book selected for inclusion. The files are processed to give a consistently clear, crisp image, and the books finished to the high quality standard for which the Press is recognised around the world. The latest print-on-demand technology ensures that the books will remain available indefinitely, and that orders for single or multiple copies can quickly be supplied.

The Cambridge Library Collection will bring back to life books of enduring scholarly value (including out-of-copyright works originally issued by other publishers) across a wide range of disciplines in the humanities and social sciences and in science and technology.

Poets and Dreamers

Studies and Translations from the Irish

Augusta Gregory

CAMBRIDGE UNIVERSITY PRESS

Cambridge, New York, Melbourne, Madrid, Cape Town, Singapore,
São Paolo, Delhi, Dubai, Tokyo, Mexico City

Published in the United States of America by Cambridge University Press, New York

www.cambridge.org
Information on this title: www.cambridge.org/9781108022040

© in this compilation Cambridge University Press 2010

This edition first published 1903
This digitally printed version 2010

ISBN 978-1-108-02204-0 Paperback

POETS AND DREAMERS

BY THE SAME WRITER

CUCHULAIN OF MUIRTHEMNE : THE STORY OF THE MEN
OF THE RED BRANCH OF ULSTER, ARRANGED AND PUT
INTO ENGLISH BY LADY GREGORY. PUBLISHED BY JOHN
MURRAY, LONDON. 6/- NET.

"In his interesting preface to Lady Gregory's *Cuchulain of Muir-themne*, Mr. W. B. Yeats expresses his opinion that it is the best book that has come from Ireland in recent years. In this we heartily concur. For the first time we have a thoroughly literary version of the 'Tain' and its cycle of tales, which may be compared, without the least misgiving, to Lady Charlotte Guest's version of the Mabinogion."—*The Times*.

"Lady Gregory has merited the undying gratitude of her countrymen and charmed the world by having once for all 'arranged and put into English the Story of the Red Branch of Ulster.' . . . In presenting this great cycle of bygone days to her own generation, Lady Gregory has worked on a method at once the most reverent and the most judicious, the most faithful and the most courageous. . . . And finally, she has discovered a beautiful and living speech, which, with the warrant of a fine old age echoing the lilt of ancient music, is yet a true English dialect entirely free from discordant archaisms. Her words are of to-day only, but so cunningly arranged in well-ordered sentences, that we seem listening to the very voice of Nature hymning Humanity."—Mr. R. Brimley Johnson in *Atlantic Monthly*.

"It is seldom that we read a new book with entire delight, or praise it without many silent reservations. It is by the nature of things more seldom still that we find ourselves enriched by a new and real possession, a treasure that will be ours for our lives, and a joy of many generations after us. But such a book in sober earnest is Lady Gregory's English version of *Cuchulain of Muirthemne*, and Mr. Yeats has not exaggerated in speaking of it as 'the best thing that has come out of Ireland' in his time, for, beautiful as his own work is, he has not yet equalled this fabric of the giants of old, massive and aerial, grotesque and exquisite beyond the power of a later and lesser generation—*Qualia nunc hominum producit corpora tellus*."—Mr. Henry Newbolt in *Monthly Review*.

POETS AND DREAMERS: STUDIES
AND TRANSLATIONS FROM THE
IRISH BY LADY GREGORY.

DUBLIN: HODGES, FIGGIS,
AND CO., LTD. LONDON:
JOHN MURRAY, ALBEMARLE
STREET. MCMIII.

TO SOME UNDERGRADUATES OF TRINITY COLLEGE

'Will you seek afar off? You surely come back at last,
' In things best known to you finding the best, or as good as
   the best ;
' In folks nearest to you finding the sweetest, strongest,
   lovingest ;
' Happiness, knowledge not in another place but this place—
   not for another hour but this hour.'

WALT WHITMAN.

CONTENTS

POETS AND DREAMERS

RAFTERY

I.

ONE winter afternoon as I sat by the fire in a ward of Gort Workhouse, I listened to two old women arguing about the merits of two rival poets they had seen and heard in their childhood.

One old woman, who was from Kilchreest, said: 'Raftery hadn't a stim of sight; and he travelled the whole nation; and he was the best poet that ever was, and the best fiddler. It was always at my father's house, opposite the big tree, that he used to stop when he was in Kilchreest. I often saw him; but I didn't take much notice of him then, being a child; it was after that I used to hear so much about him. Though he was blind, he could serve himself with his knife and fork as well as any man with his sight. I remember the way he used to cut the meat—across, like this. Callinan was nothing to him.'

The other old woman, who was from Craughwell, said: 'Callinan was a great deal better than him; and he could make songs in English as well as in

Irish; Raftery would run from where Callinan was. And he was a nice respectable man, too, with cows and sheep, and a kind man. *He* would never put anything that wasn't nice into a poem, and *he* would never run anyone down; but if you were the worst in the world, he'd make you the best in it; and when his wife lost her beetle, he made a song of fifteen verses about it.'

'Well,' the Kilchreest old woman admitted, 'Raftery would run people down; he was someway bitter; and if he had anything against a person, he'd give him a great lacerating. But there were more for him than for Callinan; some used to say Callinan's songs were too long.'

'I tell you,' said the other, 'Callinan was a nice man and a nice neighbour. Raftery wasn't fit to put beside him. Callinan was a man that would go out of his own back door, and make a poem about the four quarters of the earth. I tell you, you would stand in the snow to listen to Callinan!' But, just then, a bedridden old woman suddenly sat up and began to sing Raftery's 'Bridget Vesach' as long as her breath lasted; so the last word was for him after all.

Raftery died over sixty years ago; but there are many old people still living, besides those two old women, who have seen him, and who keep his songs in their memory. What they tell of him shows how closely he was in the old tradition of the bards, the wandering poets of two thousand years or more.

His satire, his praises, his competitions with other poets were the dread and the pride of many Galway and Mayo parishes. And now the songs that he never wrote down, being blind, are known, if not as our people say, 'all over the world,' at least in all places where Irish is spoken.

Raftery's satires, as I have heard them repeated by the country people, do not seem, even in their rhymed original—he only composed in Irish—to have the 'sharp spur' of some of his predecessors, such as O'Higinn, whose tongue was cut out by men from Sligo, who had suffered from it, or O'Daly, who criticised the poverty of the Irish chiefs in the sixteenth century until the servant of one of them stuck a knife into his throat. Yet they were much dreaded. 'He was very sharp with anyone that didn't please him,' I have been told ; 'and no one would like to be put in his songs.' And though it is said of his songs in praise of his friends that 'whoever he praised was well praised,' it was thought safer that one's own name should not appear in them. The man at whose house he died said to me : 'He used often to come and stop with us, but he never made a verse about us; my father wouldn't have liked that. Someway it doesn't bring luck.' And another man says : 'My father often told me about Raftery. He was someway gifted, and people were afraid of him. I was often told by men that gave him a lift in their car when they overtook him now and again, that if he asked their name, they wouldn't give it, for fear he might put it in a song.'

And another man says : ' There was a friend of my
father's was driving his car on the road one day, and
he saw Raftery, but he didn't let on to see him. But
when he was passing, Raftery said : " There was never
a soldier marching but would get his billet. But
the rabbit has an enemy in the ferret ; " so then the
man said in a hurry, " Oh, Mr. Raftery, I never knew
it was you : won't you get up and take a seat in the
car ? " ' A girl in whose praise he had made a song,
Mary Hynes, of Ballylee, died young, and had a
troubled life ; and one of her neighbours says of her:
' No one that has a song made about them will ever
live long ;' and another says : 'She got a great tossing
up and down ; and at last she died in the middle of a
bog.' They tell, too, of a bush that he once took shelter
under from the rain, and how he ' praised it first ; and
then when it let the rain down, he dispraised it, and
it withered up, and never put out leaf or branch after.'
I have seen his poem on the bush in a manuscript
book, carefully written in the beautiful Irish character,
and the great treasure of a stonecutter's cottage.
This is the form of the curse : ' I pronounce ugliness
upon you. That bloom or leaf may never grow on
you, but the flame of the mountain fires and of
bonfires be upon you. That you may get your
punishment from Oscar's flail, to hack and to bruise
you with the big sledge of a forge.'

There are some other verses made by him that
have been less legendary in their effect. The story
is :—' It was Anthony Daly, a carpenter, was hanged

at Seefin. It was the two Z's got him put away. He was brought before a judge in Galway, and accused of being a Captain of Whiteboys, and Mr. X, of X, swore against him that he fired at him. He was a one-eyed man; and he said: "If I did, though I have but one eye, I would have hit you"—for he was a very good shot; and he asked that some object should be put up, and he would show the judge that he would hit it, but he said nothing else. Some were afraid he'd give up the names of the other Whiteboys; but he did not. There was a gallows put up at Seefin; and he was brought there sitting on his coffin in a cart. There were people all the way along the road, and they were calling on him to break through the crowd, and they'd save him; and some of the soldiers were Irish, and they called back that if he did they'd only fire their guns in the air; but he made no attempt, but went to the gallows quiet enough. There was a man in Gort was telling me he saw it, planting potatoes he was at Seefin that day. It was in the year 1820; and Raftery was there at the hanging, and he made a song about it. The first verse of the song said: "Wasn't that the good tree, that wouldn't let any branch that was on it fall to the ground?" He meant by that that he didn't give up the names of the other Whiteboys. And at the end he called down judgment from God on the two Z's, and, if not on them, on their children. And they that had land and farms in all parts, lost it after; and all they had vanished; and the most of their children died—

only two left, one a friar, and the other living in Gort.' And quite lately I have been told by another neighbour, in corroboration, that a girl of the Z family married into a family near his home the other day, and was coldly received ; and when my neighbour asked one of the family why this was, he was told that 'those of her people that went so high ought to have gone higher'—meaning that they themselves ought to have been on the gallows ; and then he knew that Raftery's curse was still having its effect. And he had also heard that the grass had never grown again at Seefin.

This is a part of the song :—

'The evening of Friday of the Crucifixion, the Gael was under the mercy of the Gall. It was as heavy the same day as when the only Son of Mary was on the tree. I have hope in the Son of God, my grief! and it is of no use for me ; and it was Conall and his wife hung Daly, and may they be paid for it!

'But oh ! young woman, while I live, I put death on the village where you will be ; plague and death on it ; and may the flood rise over it ; that much is no sin at all, O bright God ; and I pray with longing it may fall on the man that hung Daly ; that left his people and his children crying.

'O stretch out your limbs ! The air is murky overhead ; there is darkness on the sun, and the fish do not leap in the water ; there is no dew on the grass, and the birds do not sing sweetly. With sorrow after you, Daly, till death, there never will be fruit on the trees.

'And that is the true man, that didn't humble himself or lower himself to the Gall ; Anthony Daly, O Son of God ! He was that with us always, without a lie. But he died a good Irishman ; and he never bowed the head to any man ;

and it was with false swearing that Daly was hung, and with the strength of the Gall.

'If I were a clerk—kind, light, cheerful with the pen—it is I would write your ways in clear Irish on a flag above your head. A thousand and eight hundred and sixteen, and four put to that, from the coming of the Son of God, to the death of Daly at the Castle of Seefin.'

I have heard, and have also seen in manuscript, a terrible list of curses that he hurled at the head of another poet, Seaghan Burke. But these were, I think, looked on as a mere professional display, and do not seem to have any ill effect.

Here are some of them :—

'That God may perish you on the mountain-side, without a priest, bishop, or clerk. Seven years may you be senseless and without wit, going from door to door as an unfortunate creature.

'May you have a mouth that will go back to your ear, and may your lips be turned back like gums; that your legs may lose feeling from the knee down, your eyes lose their sight, and your hands lose their strength.

'Deformity and lameness and corruption upon you; flight and defeat and the hatred of your kin. That shivering fever may stretch you nine times, and that particularly at the time of Easter' ('because,' it is explained, 'it was at Easter time our Lord was put to death, and it is the time He can best hear the curses of the poor').

'May a sore heart and cold flesh be upon you; may there be no marrow or moisture in your bones. That clay may never be put over your coffin-boards, but wind and a sharp blast on you from the north.

'Baldness and nakedness come upon you, judgment from above, and the curses of the crowd. May dragon's gall and poison mixed through it be your best drink at the hour of death.'

Sometimes he left a scathing verse on a place where he was not well treated, as: 'Oranmore without merriment. A little town in scarce fields—a broken little town, with its back to the water, and with women that have no understanding.'

He did not spare persons any more than places, especially if they were well-to-do, for his gentleness was for the poor. An old woman who remembers him says: 'He didn't care much about big houses. Just if they were people he liked, and that he was friendly with them, he would be kind enough to go in and see them.' A Mr. Burke, who met him going from his house, asked how he had fared, and he said in a scornful verse :—

> 'Potatoes that were softer than the fog,
> And with neither butter nor meat,
> And milk that was sourer than apples in harvest—
> That's what Raftery got from Burke of Kilfinn.'

'And Mr. Burke begged him to rhyme no more, but to come back, and he would be well taken care of.' I am told of another house he abused and that is now deserted: 'Frenchforth of the soot, that was wedded to the smoke, that is all that remains of the property. . . . There were some of them on mules, and some of them unruly, and the biggest of them were smaller than asses, and the master cracking them with a stick;' 'but he went no further than that, because he remembered the good treatment used to be there in former times, and he wouldn't have said that much if it wasn't for the servants that vexed him.' A satire, that is remembered in Aran, was made with the better intention of helping a barefooted girl, who had been kept waiting a long time for a pair of shoes she had ordered. Raftery came, and sat down before the shoemaker's house, and began :—

'A young little girl without sense, the ground tearing her feet, is not satisfied yet by the lying Peter Glynn. Peter Glynn, the liar, in his little house by the side of the road, is without the strength in his arms to slip together a pair of brogues.'

'And, before he had finished the lines, Peter Glynn ran out and called to him to stop, and he set at work on the shoes then and there.' He even ventured to poke a little satire at a priest sometimes. 'He went into the chapel at Kilchreest one time, and there was some cabbage after being stolen from a garden, and the priest was speaking about it. Raftery was at the bottom of the chapel, and at last he called out in verse :—" What a lot of talk about cabbage! If there was meat with it, it would feed the whole parish!" The priest didn't mind, but afterwards he came down, and said: "Where is the cabbage man?" and asked him to make some more verses about it; but whether he did or not I don't know.' And another time, I am told: 'A priest wanted to teach him the rite of lay baptism; for there were scattered houses a priest might take a long time getting to, away from the roads, and certain persons were authorized to give the rite. So the priest put his hat in Raftery's hand, and told him the words to say; but

it is what he said : " I baptize you without either foot
or hand, without salt or tow, beer or drink. Your
father was a ram and your mother was a sheep,
and your like never came to be baptized before." He
was put under a curse, too, one time by a priest, and
he made a song about him ; but he said he put his
frock out of the bargain, and it was only the priest's
own body he would speak about. And the priest let
him alone after that.' And an old basket-maker, who
had told me some of these things, said at the end :
' That is why the poets had to be banished before in
the time of St. Columcill. Sure no one could stand
the satire of them.'

II.

IRISH history having been forbidden in schools, has
been, to a great extent, learned from Raftery's poems
by the people of Mayo, where he was born, and of
Galway, where he spent his later years. It is hard to
say where history ends in them and religion and
politics begin ; for history, religion, and politics grow
on one stem in Ireland, an eternal trefoil. ' He was
a great historian,' it is said ; ' for every book he'd get
hold of, he'd get it read out to him.' And a neighbour tells me : ' He used to stop with my uncle that
was a hedge schoolmaster in those times in Ballylee,
and that was very fond of drink ; and when he was
drunk, he'd take his clothes off, and run naked
through the country. But at evening he'd open the
school ; and the neighbours that would be working all

day would gather in to him, and he'd teach them
through the night; and there Raftery would be in
the middle of them.' His chief historical poem is the
' Talk with the Bush,' of over three hundred lines.
Many of the people can repeat it, or a part of it, and
some possess it in manuscript. The bush, a fore-
runner of the ' Talking Oak ' or the ' Father of the
Forest,' gives its recollections, which go back to the
times of the Firbolgs, the Tuatha De Danaan, 'without
heart, without humanity'; the Sons of the Gael; the
heroic Fianna, who 'would never put more than one
man to fight against one'; Cuchulain 'of the Grey
Sword, that broke every gap'; till at last it comes to
' O'Rourke's wife that brought a blow to Ireland': for
it was on her account the English were first called in.
Then come the crimes of the English, made redder
by the crime of Martin Luther. Henry VIII
' turned his back on God and denied his first
wife.' Elizabeth ' routed the bishops and the Irish
Church. James and Charles laid sharp scourges on
Ireland. . . . Then Cromwell and his hosts swept
through Ireland, cutting before him all he could.
He gave estates and lands to Cromwellians, and he
put those that had a right to them on mountains.'
Whenever he brings history into his poems, the same
strings are touched. ' At the great judgment, Cromwell will be hiding, and O'Neill in the corner. And I
think if William can manage it at all, he won't stand
his ground against Sarsfield.' And a moral often
comes at the end, such as: ' Don't be without

courage, but join together ; God is stronger than the Cromwellians, and the cards may turn yet.'

For Raftery had lived through the '98 Rebellion, and the struggle for Catholic Emancipation ; and he saw the Tithe War, and the Repeal movement ; and it is natural that his poems, like those of the poets before him, should reflect the desire of his people for ' the mayntenance of their own lewde libertye,' that had troubled Spenser in his time.

Here are some verses from his '*Cuis da ple*,' 'cause to plead,' composed at the time of the Tithe War :—

'The two provinces of Munster are afoot, and will not stop till tithes are overthrown, and rents accordingly ; and if help were given them, and we to stand by Ireland, the English guard would be feeble, and every gap made easy. The Gall (English) will be on their back without ever returning again ; and the Orangemen bruised in the borders of every town, a judge and jury in the courthouse for the Catholics, England dead, and the crown upon the Gael. . . .

'There is many a fine man at this time sentenced, from Cork to Ennis and the town of Roscrea, and fair-haired boys wandering and departing from the streets of Kilkenny to Bantry Bay. But the cards will turn, and we'll have a good hand : the trump shall stand on the board we play at. . . . Let ye have courage. It is a fine story I have. Ye shall gain the day in every quarter from the Sassanach. Strike ye the board, and the cards will be coming to you, Drink out of hand now a health to Raftery : it is he would put success for you on the *Cuis da ple*.'

This is part of another song :—

· I have a hope in Christ that a gap will be opened again for us. . . . The day is not far off, the Gall will be stretched without anyone to cry after them; but with us there will be a bonfire lighted up on high. . . . The music of the world entirely, and Orpheus playing along with it. I'd sooner than all that, the Sassanach to be cut down.'

But with all this, he had plenty of common sense, and an old man at Ballylee tells me :—'One time there were a sort of nightwalkers—Moonlighters as we'd call them now, Ribbonmen they were then—making some plan against the Government; and they asked Raftery to come to their meeting. And he went; but what he said was this, in a verse, that they should look at the English Government, and think of all the soldiers it had, and all the police—no, there were no police in those days, but gaugers and such like—and they should think how full up England was of guns and arms, so that it could put down Buonaparty; and that it had conquered Spain, and took Gibraltar from it; and the same in America, fighting for twenty-one years. And he asked them what they had to fight with against all those guns and arms?—nothing but a stump of a stick that they might cut down below in the wood. So he bid them give up their nightwalking, and come out and agitate in the daylight.'

I have been told—but I do not know if it is true—that he was once sent to Galway Gaol for three months for a song he made against the Protestant Church, 'saying it was like a wall slipping, where it wasn't built solid.'

III.

WHEN, at the beginning of the seventeenth century, the poets O'Lewy and O'Clery and their supporters held a ' Contention,' the results were written down in a volume containing 7,000 lines. I think the greater number of the ' Contentions' between Raftery and his fellow-poets were never written down; but the country people still discuss them with all the eagerness of partisans. An old man from Athenry says : ' Raftery travelled Ireland, challenging all the poets of that time. There were hundreds of country poets in those days, and a welcome for them all. Raftery had enough to do to beat them, but he was the best ; his poetry was the gift of God, and his poems are sung as far away as Limerick and Dublin.' There is a story of his knocking at a door one night, when he was looking for the house of a poet he had heard of and wanted to challenge, and saying : ' I am a poet seeking shelter '; and a girl answered him from within with a verse, saying he must be a blind man to be out so late looking for shelter ; and then he knew it was the house he was looking for. And it is said that the daughter of another poet he was on his way to see in Clare, gave him such a sharp answer when he met her outside the house that he turned back and would not contend with her father at all. And he is said to have ' hunted another poet, Daly—hunted him all through Ireland.' But these other poets do not seem to have left a great name. There was a

Connemara poet, Sweeny, that was put under a curse by the priests ' because he used to make so much fun at the wakes'; and in one of Raftery's poems he thanks Sweeny for having come to his help in some dispute ; and there was 'one John Burke, who was a good poet, too ; he and Raftery would meet at fairs and weddings, and be trying which would put down the other.' I am told of an 'attack' they made on each other one day on the fair green of Cappaghtagle. Burke said : ' After all your walk of land and callows, Burke is before you at the fair of Cappagh.' And Raftery said : 'You are not Burke but a breed of *scatties*, That's all over the country gathering *praties ;* When I 'm at the table filling glasses, You are in the corner with your feet in the ashes.' Then Burke said : ' Raftery a poet, and he with bracked (speckled) shins, And he playing music with catgut ; Raftery the poet, and his back to the wall, And he playing music for empty pockets. There's no one cares for his music at all, but he does be always craving money.' For he was sometimes accused of love of money ; 'he wouldn't play for empty pockets, and he 'd make the plate rattle at the end of a dance.'

But his most serious rival in his own part of the country was Callinan, the well-to-do farmer who lived near Craughwell, of whom the old women in the workhouse spoke. I have heard some of Callinan's poems and songs ; but I do not find the imaginative power of Raftery in them. He seems, in distinction to him, to be the poet of the domestic affections, of

the settled classes. His songs have melody and good
sentiments ; and they are often accompanied by a
rhymed English version, made by his brother, a
lesser poet. The favourite among them is a song on
a wooden beetle, lost by his wife when washing clothes
at the river. She is made to lament the loss of 'so
good a servant' in a sort of allegory ; and then its
journey is traced from the river to the sea. An old
man gives me a little memory of him : 'I saw Callinan
one time when we went to dig potatoes for him at
his own place, the other side of Craughwell. We
went into the house for dinner ; and we were in a
hurry, and he was sitting by the hearth talking all
the time ; for he was a great talker, so that the veins
of his neck swelled up. And he was telling us about
the song he made about his own Missus when she
was out washing by the river. He was up to eighty
years at that time.' And there are accounts of the
making of some of his songs that show his kindly
disposition and amiability. 'One time there was a
baby in the house, and there was a dance going on
near, and Mrs. Callinan was a young woman ; and
she said she'd go for a bit to the dance-house ; and
she bid Callinan rock the cradle till she'd come back.
But she never came back till morning, and there he
was rocking the cradle still ; and he had a song composed while she was away about the time of a man's
llfe, and the hours of the day, and the seasons of the
year ; how when a man is young he is strong, and
then he grows old and passes away, and goes to the

feast of the Saviour; and about the day, how bright the morning is, and the birds singing; and a man goes out to work, and he comes in tired out, and sits by the fire to talk with his neighbour ; and the night comes on, and he says his prayers, and thinks of the feast of the Saviour ; and about the seasons, the spring so nice, and the summer for work ; and autumn brings the harvest, and winter brings Christmas, the feast of the Saviour. In Irish and English he made that.' And this is another story: ' A carpenter made a plough for Callinan one time, and when it came, it was the worst ever made ; and he said to his brother : " I 'll make a song that will cut him down altogether." But his brother said : " Do not, for if you cut him down, it will take his means of living from him, but make a song in his praise." And he did so, for he wouldn't like to do him any harm.' I have asked if he made any love-songs, and was told of one he had made 'about a girl he met going to a bog. He praised herself first, and then he said he had information as well that she had fifty gold guineas saved up.'

His having been well off seems to make his poetic merit the greater in the eyes of farmers; for one says: ' He was as good a poet, for he had a plough and horses and a good way of living, and never sang in any public-house ; but Raftery had no way of living but to go round and to mark some house to go to, and then all the neighbours would gather in to hear him.' Another says : ' Raftery was the best poet, for

C

he had nothing else to do, and laid his mind to it ; but Callinan was a strong farmer, and had other things to think of ;' and another says : 'Callinan was very apt : it was all Raftery could do to beat him ;' and another sums up by saying : 'The both of them was great.'   But a supporter of Raftery says : 'He was the best ; he put his words so strong and stiff, following one another.'

I had been often told, by supporters of either side, that there was one contest between the two, at which Callinan 'made Raftery cry tears down ;' and I wondered how it was that his wit had so far betrayed him.   It has been explained to me lately.   Raftery had made a long poem, 'The Hunt,' in which he puts 'a Writer' in the place of the fox, and calls on all the gentlemen of Galway and Mayo, and even on 'Sarsfield from Limerick,' to come and hunt him through their respective neighbourhoods with a pack of hounds.   It contains many verses ; and he seems to have improvised others in the different places where he sang it.   In the written copy I have seen, Burke is the 'Writer' who is thus hunted.   But he probably put in the name of any other rival from time to time.   This is the story : 'He and the Callinans were sometimes vexed with one another, but they'd make friends after ; but there was one day he was put down by them.   There was a funeral going on at Killeenan, and Raftery was there ; and he was asked into the corpse-house afterwards, and the people asked him for the song about Callinan ; and he began hunting him all through the country, and the people were laughing and making him go on; but Callinan's brother had come in, and was listening to him, and Raftery didn't see him, being blind; and he brought him to Killeenan at last, and he said: "Where can the rogue go now, unless he'll swim the turlough?" And at that Callinan's brother stood up and said, "Who is it you are calling a rogue?" And Raftery tried to laugh it off, and he said, "You mustn't expect poetry and truth to go together." But Callinan said: "I'll give you poetry that's truth as well;" and he began to say off some verses his brother had made on Raftery; and Raftery was choked up that time, and hadn't a word.' This story is corroborated by an eye-witness who said to me: 'It was in this house he was on the night Callinan made him cry. My father was away at the time; if he had been there, he never would have let Callinan come into the house unknown to Raftery.' I have not heard all of Callinan's poem, but this is part of it:—

'He left the County Mayo; he was hunted up from the country of the brothons' (thick bed-coverings, then made in Mayo) 'without any for the night, nor any shift for bedding, but with an old yellow blanket with a thousand patches; he had a black trouser down to the ground with two hundred holes and forty pieces; he had long legs like the shank of a pipe, and a long great coat, for it is many the dab he put in his pocket. His coat was greasy, and it was no wonder, and an old grey hat as grey as snuff, as it was many the day it was in the dunghill.'

It is said that 'Raftery could have answered that song better, but he had no back here ; and Callinan was well-to-do, and had so many of his family and so many friends.' But others say there were some allusions in it to the poverty of his home, that had become known through a servant girl from Raftery's birth-place. But I think even Callinan's friends are sorry now that Raftery was ever made to 'cry tears down.'

IV.

A MAN near Oranmore says : 'There used to be great talk of the Fianna ; and everyone had the poems about them till Raftery came, and he put them out. For when the people got Raftery's songs in their heads, they could think of nothing else : his songs put out everything else. I remember when I was a boy of ten, I was so taken up with his rhymes and songs, I had them all off. And I heard he was coming one night to a stage he had below there where he used to come now and again. And I begged my father to bring me with him that night, and he did ; but whatever happened, Raftery didn't come that time, and the next year he died.'

But it is hard to judge of the quality of Raftery's poems. Some of them have probably been lost altogether. There are already different versions of those written out in manuscript books, and of these books many have disappeared or been destroyed, and some have been taken to America by emigrants. It is said that when he was on his deathbed, he was very sorry that his songs had not all been taken down; and that he dictated one he composed there to a young man who wrote it down in Irish, but could not read his own writing when he had done, and that vexed Raftery; and then a man came in, and he asked him to take down all his songs, and he could have them for himself; but he said, 'If I did, I'd always be called Raftery,' and he went out again.

I hear the people say now and then : 'If he had had education, he would have been the greatest poet in the world.' I cannot but be sorry that his education went so far as it did, for 'he used to carry a book about with him—a Pantheon—about the heathen gods and goddesses ; and whoever he 'd get that was able to read, he 'd get him to read it to him, and then he 'd keep them in his mind, and use them as he wanted them.' If he had been born a few decades later, he would have been caught, like other poets of the time, in the formulas of English verse. As it was, both his love poems and his religious poems were caught in the formulas imported from Greece and from Rome ; and any formula must make a veil between the prophet who has been on the mountain top, and the people who are waiting at its foot for his message. The dreams of beauty that formed themselves in the mind of the blind poet become flat and vapid when he embodies them in the well-worn names of Helen and Venus. The truths of God that he strove in his last years, as he says, 'to have written in the book of the people,' left those unkindled whose ears were already wearied with the well-known words 'the keys of Heaven,' 'penance, fasts, and alms,' to whom it was an old tale to hear of hell as a furnace, and the grave as a dish for worms. When he gets away from the formulas, he has often a fine line on death or on judgment; the cheeks of the dead are 'cold as the snow that is at the back of the sun ;' the careless—those who 'go out looking at their sheep on Sunday instead of going to Mass'—are warned that 'on the side of the hill of the tears there will be Ochone!'

His love songs are many; and they were not always thought to bring ill luck ; for I am told of a girl 'that was not handsome at all, but ugly, that he made a song about her for civility; for she used to be in a house where he used to lodge, and the song got her a husband ; and there is a son of hers living now down in Clare-Galway.' And an old woman tells me, with a sigh of regret for what might have been, that she saw Raftery one time at a dance, and he spoke to her and said : 'Well planed you are ; the carpenter that planed you knew his trade.' 'And I said : "Better than you know yours;" for there were two or three of the strings of his fiddle broke. And then he said something about O'Meara, that lived near us; and my father got vexed at what he said, and would let him speak no more with me. And if it wasn't for him speaking about O'Meara, and my father getting vexed, he might have made words about me like he did for Mary Hynes and for Mary Brown.'

'Bridget Vesach,' which I have heard in many cottages, as well as from the old woman in Gort Workhouse, begins : 'I would wed courteous Bridget without coat, shoe, or shirt. Treasure of my heart, if it were possible for me, I would fast for you nine meals, without food, without drink, without any share of anything, on an island of Lough Erne, with desire for you and me to be together till we should settle our case. . . . My heart started with trouble, and I was frightened nine times that morning that I heard you were not to be found. . . . I would sooner be stretched by you with nothing under us but heather and rushes, than be listening to the cuckoos that are stirring at the break of day. . . . I am in grief and in sorrow since you slipped from me across the mearings.'

Another love poem, 'Mairin Stanton,' shows his habit of mixing comparisons drawn from the classics with those drawn from nature :—

'There's a bright flower by the side of the road, and she beats Deirdre in the beauty of her voice; or I might say Helen, Queen of the Greeks, she for whose sake hundreds died at Troy.

'There is light and brightness in her as in those others; her little mouth is as sweet as the cuckoo on the branch. You would not find a mind like hers in any woman since the pearl died that was in Ballylee.

'To see under the sky a woman settled like her walking on the road on a fine sunny day, the light flashing from the whiteness of her breast would give sight to a man without eyes.

'There is the love of hundreds in her face, and there is the promise of the evening star. If she had been living in the time of the gods, it is not Venus that would have had the apple.

'Her hair falls down below her knees, waving and winding to the mouth of her shoes; her locks spread out wide and pale like dew, they leave a brightness on the road behind her.

'She is the girl that has been taught the nicest of all whose eyes still open to the sun; and if the estate of Lord Lucan belonged to me, on the strength of my cause this jewel would be mine.

'Her slender lime-white shape, her face like flowers, her neck, her cheek, and her amber hair; Virgil, Cicero, and Homer could tell of nothing like her; she is like the dew in the time of harvest.

'If you could see this plant moving or dancing, you could not but love the flower of the branch. If I cannot get a hundred words with Mairin Stanton, I do not think my life will last long.

'She said "Good morrow" early and pleasantly; she drank my health, and gave me a stool, and it not in the corner. At the time that I am ready to go on my way I will stay talking and talking with her.'

The 'pearl that was at Ballylee' was poor Mary Hynes, of whom I have already spoken. His song on her is very popular; 'a great song, so that her name is sung through the three parishes.' She must have been beautiful, for many who knew her still speak of her beauty, of her long, shining hair, and the 'little blushes in her cheeks.' An old woman says: 'I never can think of her but I'll get a trembling, she was so nice; and if she was to begin talking, she'd

keep you laughing till daybreak.' But others say: ' It
was the poet that made her so handsome'; or, 'whatever she was, he made twice as much of it.' I give
one or two verses of the song :—

'There was no part of Ireland I did not travel : from the
rivers to the tops of the mountains, to the edge of Lough
Greine, whose mouth is hidden; but I saw no beauty but
was behind hers.
' Her hair was shining, and her brows were shining too ; her
face was like herself, her mouth pleasant and sweet. She is
the pride, and I give her the branch. She is the shining
flower of Ballylee.'

Even many miles from Ballylee, if the *posin
glégeal*—the 'shining flower'—is spoken of, it is
always known that it is Mary Hynes who is meant.

Raftery is said to have spent the last seven years
of his life praying and making religious songs, because
death had told him in a vision that he had only seven
years to live. His own account of the vision was
given me by the man at whose house he died. ' I
heard him telling my father one time, that he was
sick in Galway, and there was a mug beside the bed,
and in the night he heard a noise, and he thought it
was the cat was on the table, and that she'd upset
the mug ; and he put his hand out, and what he felt
was the bones and the thinness of death. And his
sight came to him, and he saw where his wrapper was
hanging on the wall. And death said he had come
to bring him away, or else one of the neighbours that
lived in such a house. And after they had talked

a while, he said he would give him a certain time
before he'd come for him again, and he went away.
And in the morning when his wife came in, he asked
where did she hang his wrapper the night before, and
she told him it was in such a place, and that was the
very place he saw it, so he knew he had had his sight.
And then he sent to the house that had been spoken
of to know how was the man of it, and word came
back that he was dead.   I remember when he was
dying, a friend of his, one Cooney, came in to see
him, and said: "Well, Raftery, the time is not up yet
that death gave you to live."   And he said: " The
Church and myself have it made out that it was not
death that was there, but the devil that came to
tempt me." '

His description of death in his poem on the
' Vision,' is vivid and unconventional :—

' I had a vision in my sleep last night, between sleeping and
waking, a figure standing beside me, thin, miserable, sad, and
sorrowful ; the shadow of night upon his face, the tracks of the
tears down his cheeks.   His ribs were bending like the bottom
of a riddle ; his nose thin, that it would go through a cambric
needle ; his shoulders hard and sharp, that they would cut
tobacco ; his head dark and bushy like the top of a hill ; and
there is nothing I can liken his fingers to.   His poor bones
without any kind of covering ; a withered rod in his hand, and
he looking in my face.   It is not worth my while to be talking
about him ; I questioned him in the name of God.'

A long conversation follows ; Raftery addresses
him :—

' Whatever harbour you came from last night, move up to
me and speak if you can.'   Death answers: "Put away Hebrew,

Greek and Latin, French, and the three sorts of English, and I will speak to you sweetly in Irish, the language that you found your verses in. I am death that has hidden hundreds: Hannibal, Pompey, Julius Cæsar; I was in the way with Queen Helen. I made Hector fall, that conquered the Greeks, and Conchubar, that was king of Ireland; Cuchulain and Goll, Oscar and Diarmuid, and Oisin, that lived after the Fenians; and the children of Usnach that brought away Deirdre from Conchubar; at a touch from me they all fell." But Raftery answers: "O high Prince, without height, without followers, without dwelling, without strength, without hands, without force, without state: all in the world wouldn't make me believe it, that you'd be able to put down the half of them." '

But death speaks solemnly to him then, and warns him that :—

'Life is not a thing that you get a lease of; there will be stones and a sod over you yet. Your ears that were so quick to hear everything will be closed, deaf, without sound, without hearing; your tongue that was so sweet to make verses will be without a word in the same way. . . . Whatever store of money or wealth you have, and the great coat up about your ears, death will snap you away from the middle of it." '

And the poem ends at last with the story of the Passion and a prayer for mercy.

He was always ready to confess his sins with the passionate exaggeration of St. Paul or of Bunyan. In his 'Talk with the Bush,' when a flood is threatened, he says :—

'I was thinking, and no blame to me, that my lease of life wouldn't be long, and that it was bad work my hands had left after them; to be committing sins since I was a child, swearing big oaths and blaspheming. I never think to go to Mass. Confession at Christmas I wouldn't ask to go to. I would laugh at my neighbour's downfall, and I'd make nothing of breaking the Ten Commandments. Gambling and drinking and all sorts of pleasures that would come across me, I'd have my hand in them.'

The poem known as his 'Repentance' is in the same strain. It is said to have been composed 'one time he went to confession to Father Bartley Kilkelly, and he refused him absolution because he was too much after women and drink. And that night he made up his "Repentance"; and the next day he went again, and Father Pat Burke, the curate, was with Father Bartley, and he said: "Well, Raftery, what have you composed of late?" and he said: "This is what I composed," and he said the Repentance. And then Father Bartley said to the curate: "You may give him absolution, where he has his repentance made before the world."'

It is one of the finest of his poems. It begins:—

'O King, who art in heaven, . . . I scream to Thee again and again aloud, For it is Thy grace I am hoping for.

'I am in age, and my shape is withered; many a day I have been going astray. . . . When I was young, my deeds were evil; I delighted greatly in quarrels and rows. I liked much better to be playing or drinking on a Sunday morning than to be going to Mass. . . . I was given to great oaths, and I did not let lust or drunkenness pass me by. . . . The day has stolen away, and I have not raised the hedge until the crop in which Thou didst take delight is destroyed. . . . I am a worthless stake in a corner of a hedge, or I am like a boat that has lost its rudder, that would be broken against a rock in the sea, and that would be drowned in the cold waves.'

But in spite of this self-denunciation, people who knew him say 'there was no harm in him'; though it it is added : 'but as to a drop of drink, he was fond of that to the end.' And in another mood, in his 'Argument with Whisky,' he claims, as an excuse for this weakness, the desire for companionship felt by a wanderer. 'And the world knows it's not for love of what I drink, but for love of the people that do be near me.' And he has always a confident belief in final absolution :—" I pray to you to hear me, O Son of God ; as you created the moon, the sun, the stars, it is no task or trouble for you to ready me.'

There are some fine verses in a poem made at the time of an outbreak of cholera :—

'Look at him who was yesterday swift and strong, who would leap stone wall, ditch and gap, who was in the evening walking the street, and is going under the clay on the morrow.

'Death is quicker than the wave of drowning or than any horse, however fast, on the racecourse. He would strike a goal against the crowd ; and no sooner is he there than he is on guard before us.

'He is changing, hindering, rushing, starting, unloosed ; the day is no better to him than the night ; when a person thinks there is no fear of him, there he is on the spot laid low with keening.

'Death is a robber who heaps together kings, high princes, and country lords ; he brings with him the great, the young, and the wise, gripping them by the throat before all the people.

' It is a pity for him who is tempted with the temptations of the world ; and the store that will go with him is so weak, and his lease of life no better if he were to live for a thousand years, than just as if he had slipped over on a visit and back again.

' When you are going to lie down, don't be dumb.   Bare your knee and bruise the ground.   Think of all the deeds that you put by you, and that you are travelling towards the meadow of the dead.'

Some of his poems of places, usually places in Mayo, the only ones he had ever looked on—for smallpox took his sight away in his childhood— have much charm. ' Cnocin Saibhir,' ' the Plentiful Little Hill,' must have sounded like a dream of Tir-nan-og to many a poor farmer in a sodden-thatched cottage :—

' After the Christmas, with the help of Christ, I will never stop if I am alive ; I will go to the sharp-edged little hill ; for it is a fine place, without fog falling ; a blessed place that the sun shines on, and the wind doesn't rise there or any thing of the sort.

' And if you were a year there, you would get no rest, only sitting up at night and eternally drinking.

' The lamb and the sheep are there ; the cow and the calf are there ; fine lands are there without heath and without bog. Ploughing and seed-sowing in the right month, and plough and harrow prepared and ready ; the rent that is called for there, they have means to pay it.   There is oats and flax and large-eared barley. . . . There are beautiful valleys with good growth in them, and hay.   Rods grow there, and bushes and tufts, white fields are there, and respect for trees ; shade and shelter from wind and rain ; priests and friars reading their book ; spending and getting is there, and nothing scarce.'

In another song in the same manner on 'Cilleaden,' he says :—

'I leave it in my will that my heart rises as the wind rises, or as the fog scatters, when I think upon Carra and the two towns below it, on the two-mile bush, and on the plains of Mayo. . . . And if I were standing in the middle of my people, age would go from me, and I would be young again.'

He writes of friends that he has made in Galway as well as in Mayo, a weaver, a carpenter, a priest at Kilcolgan who is 'the good Christian, the clean wheat of the Gael, the generous messenger, the standing tree of the clergy.' Some of his eulogies both on persons and places are somewhat spoiled by grotesque exaggeration. Even Cilleaden has not only all sorts of native fishes, 'as plenty as turf,' and all sorts of native trees, but is endowed with 'tortoises,' with 'logwood and mahogany.' His country weaver must not only have frieze and linen in his loom, but satin and cambric. A carpenter near Ardrahan, Seaghan Conroy, is praised with more simplicity for his 'quick, lucky work,' and for the pleasure he takes in it. 'I never met his master ; the trade was in his nature' ; and he gives a long list of all the things he could make : 'doors and all that would be wanted for a big house' ; mills and ploughs and spinning-wheels 'nicely finished with a clean chisel'; 'all sorts of things for the living, and a coffin for the dead.' And with all this 'he cares little for money, but to spend, as he earns, decently. And if he was up for nine nights, you wouldn't see the sign of a drop on him.'

Another of his more simple poems is what Spenser would call an ' elegie or friend's passion' on a player on fiddle or pipes, Thomas O'Daly, that gives him a touch of kinship with the poets who have mourned their Astrophel, their Lycidas, their Adonais, their Thyrsis. This is how I have been helped to put it into English by a young working farmer, sitting by a turf fire one evening, when his day in the fields was over :—

' It was Thomas O'Daly that roused up young people and scattered them, and since death played on him, may God give him grace.   The country is all sorrowful, always talking, since their man of sport died that would win the goal in all parts with his music.

' The swans on the water are nine times blacker than a blackberry since the man died from us that had pleasantness on the top of his fingers.   His two grey eyes were like the dew of the morning that lies on the grass.   And since he was laid in the grave, the cold is getting the upper hand.

' If you travel the five provinces, you would not find his equal for countenance or behaviour, for his equal never walked on land or grass.   High King of Nature, you who have all powers in yourself, he that wasn't narrow-hearted, give him shelter in heaven for it.

' He was the beautiful branch.   In every quarter that he ever knew he would scatter his fill and not gather.   He would spend the estate of the Dalys, their beer and their wine.   And that he may be sitting in the chair of grace, in the middle of Paradise.

' A sorrowful story on death, it's he is the ugly chief that did treachery, that didn't give him credit, O strong God, for a little time.

' There are young women, and not without reason, sorry and heart-broken and withered, since he was left at the church. Their hair thrown down and hanging, turned grey on their head.

'No flower in any garden, and the leaves of the trees have leave to cry, and they falling on the ground. There is no green flower on the tops of the tufts, since there did a boarded coffin go on Daly.

'There is sorrow on the men of mirth, a clouding over the day, and no trout swim in the river. Orpheus on the harp, he lifted up everyone out of their habits; and he that stole what Argus was watching the time he took away Io; Apollo, as we read, gave them teaching, and Daly was better than all these musicians.

'A hundred wouldn't be able to put together his actions and his deeds and his many good works. And Raftery says this much for Daly, because he liked him.'

Though his praises are usually all for the poor, for the people, he has left one beautiful lament for a landowner :—

'There's no dew or grass on Cluan Leathan. The cuckoo is not to be seen on the furze; the leaves are withering and the trees complaining of the cold. There is no sun or moon in the air or in the sky, or no light in the stars coming down, with the stretching of O'Kelly in the grave.

'My grief to tell it! he to be laid low; the man that did not bring grief or trouble on any heart, that would give help to those that were down.

'No light on the day like there was; the fruits not growing; no children on the breast; there's no return in the grain; the plants don't blossom as they used since O'Kelly with the fair hair went away; he that used to forgive us a great share of the rent.

'Since the children of Usnach and Deirdre went to the grave and Cuchulain, who, as the stories tell us, would gain victory in every step he would take; since he died, such a story never came of sorrow or defeat; since the Gael were sold at Aughrim, and since Owen Roe died, the Branch.'

D

V.

HIS life was always the wandering, homeless life of the old bards. After Cromwell's time, as the houses they went to grew poorer, they had added music to their verse-making; and Raftery's little fiddle helped to make him welcome in the Ireland which was, in spite of many sorrows, as merry and light-hearted u p to the time of the great famine as England had been up to the time of the Puritans. ' He had no place of his own,' I am told, ' but to be walking the country. He did well to die before the bad years came. He used to play at Kiltartan cross for the dancing of a Sunday evening. And when he 'd come to any place, the people would gather and he 'd give them a dance ; for there was three times as many people in the world then as what there is now. The people would never have let him want; but as to money, what could he do with it, and he with no place of his own ?' An old woman near Craughwell says : ' He used to come here often; it was like home to him. He wouldn't have a dance then; my father liked better to be sitting listening to his talk and his stories; only when we 'd come in, he 'd take the fiddle and say : " Now we must give the youngsters a tune." ' And an old man, who is still lamenting the fall in prices after the Battle of Waterloo, remembers having seen him ' one time at a shebeen house that used to be down there in Clonerle. He was playing the fiddle, and there used to be two couples at a time dancing ;

and they would put two halfpence in the plate, and
Raftery would rattle them and say : " It 's good for
the two sorts to be together," and there would be
great laughing.' And it is also said 'there was a
welcome before him in every house he 'd come to ; and
wherever he went, they 'd think the time too short
he would be with them.' There is a story I often
hear told about the marriage near Cappaghtagle of a
poor servant boy and girl, ' that was only a marriage
and not a wedding, till Raftery chanced to come in ;
and he made it one. There wasn't a bit but bread and
herrings in the house ; but he made a great song
about the grand feast they had, and he put every sort
of thing into the song—all the beef that was in Ireland ;
and went to the Claddagh, and didn't leave a fish in the
sea. And there was no one at all at it ; but he brought
all the *bacachs* and poor men in Ireland, and gave
them a pound each. He went to bed after, without
them giving him a drop to drink ; but he didn't mind
that when they hadn't got it to give.'

The wandering, unrestrained life was probably to
his mind ; and I do not think there is a word of dis-
content or complaint in any of his verses, though he
was always poor, and must often have known
hardship. In the ' Talk with the Bush,' he describes
in his whimsical, exaggerated way, a wetting, which
must have been one of very many.

' It chanced that I was travelling and the rain was heavy ;
I stepped aside, and not without reason, till I 'd get a wall or
a bush that would shelter me.

D 2

'I didn't meet at the side of a gap only an old, withered, miserable bush by the side of the wall, and it bent with the west wind. I stepped under it, and it was a wet place ; torrents of rain coming down from all quarters, east and west and straight downwards ; its equal I couldn't see, unless it is seeds winnowed through a riddle. It was sharp, angry, fierce, and stormy, like a deer running and racing past me. The storm was drowning the country, and my case was pitiful, and I suffering without cause.

'An hour and a quarter it was raining ; there isn't a drop that fell but would fill a quart and put a heap on it afterwards ; there's not a wheat or rape mill in the neighbourhood but it would set going in the middle of a field.'

At last relief comes :—

'It was shortly then the rain grew weak, the sun shone, and the wind rose. I moved on, and I smothered and drowned in wet, till I came to a little house, and there was a welcome before me. Many quarts of water I squeezed from my skirt and my cape. I hung my hat on a nail, and I lying in a sweet flowery bed. But I was up again in a little while. We began sports and pleasures ; and it was with pride we spent the night.'

But there is a verse in his 'Argument with Whisky' that seems to have a wistful thought in it, perhaps of the settled home of his rival, Callinan :—

'Cattle is a nice thing for a man to have, and his share of land to reap wheat and barley. Money in the chest, and a fire in the evening time ; and to be able to give shelter to a man on his road ; a hat and shoes in the fashion—I think, indeed, that would be much better than to be going from place to place drinking *uisge beatha*.'

And there is a little sadness in the verses he made

in some house, when a stranger asked who he was :—

'I am Raftery the poet, full of hope and love ; with eyes without light, with gentleness without misery.

'Going west on my journey with the light of my heart; weak and tired to the end of my road.

'I am now, and my back to a wall, playing music to empty pockets.'

'He was a thin man,' I am told by one who knew him, 'not very tall, with a long frieze coat and corduroy trousers. He was very strong ; and he told my father there was never any man he wrestled with but he could throw him, and that he could lie on his back and throw up a bag with four hundred of wheat in it, and take it up again. He couldn't see a stim ; but he would walk all the roads, and give the right turn, without ever touching the wall. My father was wondering at him one time they were out together; and he said : "Wait till we come to the turn to Athenry, and don't tell me of it, and see if I don't make it out right." And sure enough, when they came to it, he gave the right turn, and just in the middle.' This is explained by   —' There was a blind piper what another man tells me :— they set out together to go to Ballylee, and it was late, and they couldn't find the stile that led down there, near Early's house. And they would have stopped there till somebody would come by, but Raftery said he'd go back to Gort and step it again ; and so he did, turned back a mile to Gort, and started from

there. He counted every step that he stepped out;
and when he got to the stile, he stopped straight
before it.' And I was told also there used to be a
flagstone put beside the bog-holes to leap from, and
Raftery would leap as well as any man. He would
count his steps back from the flag, and take a run
and alight on the other side.

VI.

HIS knowledge and his poetic gift are often sup-
posed to have been given to him by the invisible
powers, who grow visible to those who have lost their
earthly sight. An old woman who had often danced
to his music, said :—'When he went to his rest at
night, it's then he'd make the songs in the turn of a
hand, and you would wonder in the morning where
he got them.' And a man who 'was too much taken
up with sport and hurling when he was a boy to
think much about him,' says : 'He got the gift. It's
said he was asked which would he choose, music or
the talk. If he chose music, he would have been
the greatest musician in the world ; but he chose the
talk, and so he was a great poet. Where could he
have found all the words he put in his songs if it
wasn't for that?' An old woman, who is more
orthodox, says :—'I often used to see him when I
was a little child, in my father's house at Corker.
He'd often come in there, and here to Coole House
he used to come as well. He couldn't see a stim,

and that is why he had such great knowledge. God gave it to him. And his songs have gone all through the world ; and he had a voice that was like the wind.'

Legends are already growing up about his death. It has been said that 'he knew the very day his time would be up; and he went to Galway, and brought a plank to the house he was stopping at, and he put it in the loft; and he told the people of the house his time was come, and bid them make a coffin for him with the plank—and he was dead before morning.' And another story says he died alone in an empty house, and that flames were seen about the house all night; and ' the flames were the angels waking him.' But many told me he had died in the house of a man near Craughwell; and one autumn day I went there to look for it, and the first person I asked was able to tell me that the house where Raftery had died was the other side of Craughwell, a mile and a half away. It was a warm, hazy day; and as I walked along the flat, deserted road that Raftery had often walked, I could see few landmarks—only a few more grey rocks, or a few more stunted hazel bushes in one stone-walled field than in another. At last I came to a thatched cottage; and when I saw an old man sitting outside it, with hat and coat of the old fashion, I felt sure it was he who had been with Raftery at the last. He was ready to talk about him, and told me how he had come there to die. ' I was a young chap at that time. It must have been in the

year 1835, for my father died in '36, and I think it
was a year before him that Raftery died.   What did
he die of ?   Of weakness.   He had been bet up in
Galway with some fit of sickness he had ; and then
he came to gather a little money about the country,
and when he got here he was bet up again.   He
wasn't an old man—only about seventy years.   He
was in the bed for about a fortnight.   When he got
bad, my father said it was best get a priest for
him ; but the parish priest was away.   But we saw
Father Nagle passing the road, and I went out and
brought him in, and he gave him absolution, and
anointed him.   He had no pain ; only his feet were
cold, and the boys used to be warming a stone in the
fire and putting it to them in the bed.   My mother
wanted to send to Galway, where his wife and his
daughter and his son were stopping, so that they
would come and care him ; but he wouldn't have them.
Someway he didn't think they treated him well.'

I had been told that the priest had refused him
absolution when he was dying, until he forgave some
enemy ; and that he had said afterwards, ' If I forgave
him with my mouth, I didn't with my heart ' ; but
this was not true.   ' Father Nagle made no delay in
anointing him ; but there was a carpenter down the
road there he said too much to, and annoyed him
one time ; and the carpenter had a touch of the poet
too, and was a great singer, and he came out and beat
him, and broke his fiddle ; and I remember when he
was dying, the priest bringing in the carpenter, and

making them forgive one another, and shake hands;
and the carpenter said: " If two brothers were to have
a falling out, they'd forgive one another—and why
wouldn't we?" He was buried in Killeenan; it wasn't
a very big funeral, but all the people of the village
came to it. He used often to come and stop with
us. . . . It was of a Christmas Eve he died; and
he had always said that, if God had a hand in it, it
was of a Christmas Day he'd die.'

I went to Killeenan to look for his grave. There
is nothing to mark it ; but two old men who had been
at his funeral pointed it out to me. There is a ruined
church in the graveyard, which is crowded ; 'there are
people killing one another now to get a place in it.'
I was asked into a house close by ; and its owner said
with almost a touch of jealousy ; 'I think it was
coming in here Raftery was the time he died ; but
he got bet up, and turned in at the house below. It
was of a Christmas Eve he died, and that shows
he was blessed ; there's a blessing on them that die
at Christmas. It was at night he was buried, for
Christmas Day no work could be done, but my father
and a few others made a little gathering to pay for a
coffin, and it was made by a man in the village on
St. Stephen's Day; and then he was brought here, and
the people from the villages followed him, for they all
had a wish for Raftery. But night was coming on
when they got here ; and in digging the grave there
was a big stone in it, and the boys thought they would
put him in a barn and take the night out of him.

But my mother—the Lord have mercy on her—had a great veneration for Raftery; and she sent out two mould candles lighted; for in those days the women used to have their own mould, and to make their own candles for Christmas. And we held the candles there where the grave is, near the gable end of the church; and my brother went down in the grave and got the stone out, and we buried him. And there was a sharp breeze blowing at the time, but it never quenched the candles or moved the flame of them, and that shows that the Lord had a hand in him.'

He and all the neighbours were glad to hear that there is soon to be a stone over the grave. 'He is worthy of it; he is well worthy of it,' they kept saying. A man who was digging sand by the roadside, took me to his house, and his wife showed me a little book, in which the 'Repentance' and other poems had been put down for her, in phonetic Irish, by a beggar who had once stayed in the house. 'Many who go to America hear Raftery's songs sung out there,' they told me with pride.

As I went back along the silent road, there was suddenly a sound of horses and a rushing and waving about me, and I found myself in the midst of the County Galway Fox Hounds, coming back from cub-hunting. The English M.F.H. and his wife rode by; and I wondered if they had ever heard of the poet whose last road this had been. Most likely not; for it is only among the people that his name has been kept in remembrance.

There is still a peasant poet here and there, making songs in the 'sweet Irish tongue,' in which death spoke to Raftery; and I think these will be held in greater honour as the time of awakening goes on. But the nineteenth century has been a time of swift change in many countries; and in looking back on that century in Ireland, there seem to have been two great landslips—the breaking of the continuity of the social life of the people by the famine, and the breaking of the continuity of their intellectual life by the shoving out of the language. It seems as if there were no place left now for the wandering versemaker, and that Raftery may have closed the long procession that had moved unbroken during so many centuries, on its journey to ' the meadow of the dead.'

1900.

It was after I had written this that I went to see Raftery's birthplace, Cilleaden, in the County Mayo.

A cousin of his came to see me, and some other men, but none of them remembered him; but they were very proud of his song on Cilleaden, which ' is all through the world.' An old woman told me she had heard it in a tramcar in America; and an old man said: 'I was coming back from England one time, and there were a lot of Irish-speaking boys from Galway on board. There was one of them sick all through the night, but he was well in the morning; and the others came round him and asked him for a song, and the song he gave was 'Cilleaden.'

They did not seem to know many of his other songs, except the 'Repentance,' which someone remembered having seen sold as a ballad, with the English on one side and the Irish on the other. And one man told me : ' The first song Raftery wrote was about a hat that was stole from a man that was working in that middle field beyond. When the man was digging, he used to put his hat on a stick in the field to frighten away the crows ; and Raftery got someone to bring away the hat, to make fun of the man. And then he made a song, making out it was the fairies had taken it ; and he made the man follow them to Cruachmaa, and from that to Roscommon, and tell all that happened him there.'

And one of them told me : ' He was six years old when the smallpox took his sight from him ; and he was marked very little by the pox, only three or four little marks—it seemed to settle in his eyes. His father was a cottier—there were many here in those times. His mother was a Brennan. There are cousins of his living yet ; but in the schools they are Englished into Rochford.'

A young man said he had been told Raftery was born in some place beyond, at the foot of the mountain, but the others were very indignant ; one got very angry, and said : ' Don't I know where he was born, and my father was the one age with him, and they sisters' sons ; and isn't Michael Conroy there below his cousin ? and it 's up in that field was the house he was born in, so don't be trying to bring him away to the mountain.'

I went to see the birthplace, a very green field with two thorn bushes growing close together by a stone. The field is called ' Sean Straid '—the old street—for a few cottages had stood there. A man who lives close by told me he had dug up a blackened stone just there, and a stone into which a bar had been let, to hang a pot on ; and that may have been the very hearth where Raftery had sat as a child.

I found one old man who remembered him. ' He used to come to my father's house often, mostly from Easter to Whitsuntide, when the cakes were made, and there would be music and dancing. He used to play the fiddle for Frank Taafe that lived here, when he would be going out riding, and the horse used to prance when he heard it. And he made verses against one Seaghan Bradach, that used to be paid thirteen pence for every head of cattle he found straying in the Jordan's fields, and used to drive them in himself. There was another poet called Devine that praised Seaghan Bradach ; and a verse was made against him again by a woman-poet that lived here at the time.'

There is a stone over Raftery's grave now ; and the people about Killeenan gather there on a Sunday in August every year to do honour to his memory. This year they established a *Feis* ; and there were prizes given for traditional singing, and for old poems repeated, and old stories told, all in the Irish tongue.

And the *Craoibhin Aoibhin* is printing week by week all of Raftery's poems that can be found, with translations, and we shall soon have them in a book.

And he has written a little play, having Raftery for its subject; and at a Galway Feis this year he himself acted, and took the blind poet's part; and he will act it many times again, *le congnamh De*—with the help of God.

1902.

WEST IRISH BALLADS

IT was only a few years ago, when Douglas Hyde published his literal translations of Connacht Love Songs, that I realized that, while I had thought poetry was all but dead in Ireland, the people about me had been keeping up the lyrical tradition that existed in Ireland before Chaucer lived. While I had been looking in the columns of Nationalist newspapers for some word of poetic promise, they had been singing songs of love and sorrow in the language that has been pushed nearer and nearer to the western seaboard—the edge of the world. 'Eyes have we, but we see not ; ears have we, but we do not understand.' It does not comfort me to think how many besides myself, having spent a lifetime in Ireland, must make this confession.

The ballads to be gathered now are a very few out of the great mass of traditional poetry that was swept away during the last century in the merciless sweeping away of the Irish tongue, and of all that was bound up with it, by England's will, by Ireland's need, by official pedantry.

To give an idea of the ballads of to-day, I will not quote from the translations of Douglas Hyde or of

Dr. Sigerson already published. I will rather give a few of the more homely ballads, sung and composed by the people, and, as far as I know, not hitherto translated.

Those I have heard since I have begun to look for them in the cottages, are, for the most part, sad ; but not long ago I heard a girl sing a merry one, in a mocking tone, about a boy on the mountain, who neglected the girls of his village to run after a strange girl from Galway ; and the girls of the village were vexed, and they made a song about him; and he went to Galway after her, and there she laughed at him, and said he had never gone to school or to the priest, and she would have nothing to do with him. So then he went back to the village, and asked the smith's daughter to marry him ; but she said she would not, and that he might go back to the strange girl from Galway. Another song I have heard was a lament over a boy and girl who had run away to America, and on the way the ship went down. And when they were going down, they began to be sorry they were not married ; and to say that if the priest had been at home when they went away, they would have been married ; but they hoped that when they were drowned, it would be the same with them as if they were married. And I heard another lament that had been made for three boys that had lately been drowned in Galway Bay. It is the mother who is making it ; and she tells how she lost her husband, the father of her three boys. And then she married

again, and they went to sea and were drowned; and
she wouldn't mind about the others so much, but it is
the eldest boy, Peter, she is grieving for. And I have
heard one song that had a great many verses, and was
about 'a poet that is dying, and he confessing his sins.'

The first ballad I give deals with sorrow and defeat
and death; for sorrow is never far from song in
Ireland; and the names best praised and kept in
memory are of those—

> ' Lonely antagonists of destiny
> That went down scornful under many spears;
> Who soon as we are born are straight our friends,
> And live in simple music, country songs,
> And mournful ballads by the winter fire.'

In this simple lament, the type of a great many,
only the first name of the young man it was made for
is given: ' Fair-haired Donough.' It is likely the
people of his own place know still to what family he
belonged; but I have not heard it sung, and only
know that he was 'some Connachtman that was
hanged in Galway.' And it is clear it was for
some political crime he was hanged, by the sugges-
tion that if he had been tried nearer his own home,
' in the place he had a right to be,' the issue would
have been different, and by the allusion to the Gall,
the English :—

> ' It was bound fast here you saw him, and you wondered to
>   see him,
> Our fair-haired Donough, and he after being condemned;
> There was a little white cap on him in place of a hat,
> And a hempen rope in the place of a neckcloth.

E

' I am after walking here all through the night,
Like a young lamb in a great flock of sheep;·
My breast open, my hair loosened out,
And how did I find my brother but stretched before me!

' The first place I cried my fill was at the top of the lake;
The second place was at the foot of the gallows ;
The third place was at the head of your dead body
Among the Gall, and my own head as if cut in two.

' If you were with me in the place you had a right to be,
Down in Sligo or down in Ballinrobe,
It is the gallows would be broken, it is the rope would be cut,
And fair-haired Donough going home by the path.

' O fair-haired Donough, it is not the gallows was fit for you ;
But to be going to the barn, to be threshing out the straw ;
To be turning the plough to the right hand and to the left,
To be putting the red side of the soil uppermost.

' O fair-haired Donough, O dear brother,
It is well I know who it was took you away from me ;
Drinking from the cup, putting a light to the pipe,
And walking in the dew in the cover of the night.

' O Michael Malley, O scourge of misfortune !
My brother was no calf of a vagabond cow ;
But a well-shaped boy on a height or a hillside,
To knock a low pleasant sound out of a hurling-stick.

' And fair-haired Donough, is not that the pity,
You that would carry well a spur or a boot ;
I would put clothes in the fashion on you from cloth that
    would be lasting ;
I would send you out like a gentleman's son.

' O Michael Malley, may your sons never·be in one another's
    company ;
May your daughters never ask a marriage portion of you ;
The two ends of the table are empty, the house is filled,
And fair-haired Donough, my brother, is stretched out.

' There is a marriage portion coming home for Donough,
But it is not cattle nor sheep nor horses ;
But tobacco and pipes and white candles,
And it will not be begrudged to them that will use it.'

A very pathetic touch is given by the idea of the
' marriage portion,' the provision for the wake, being
brought home for the dead boy.

But it is chiefly in Aran, and on the opposite
Connemara coast, that Irish ballads are still being
made as well as sung. The little rock islands of
Aran are fit strongholds for the threatened language,
breakwaters of Europe, taking as they do the first
onset of the ocean 'that hath no limits nearer than
America.' The fisher-folk go out in their canvas
curraghs to win a living from the Atlantic, or pain-
fully carry loads of sand and seaweed to make the
likeness of an earth-plot on the bare rock. The
Irish coast seems far away ; the setting sun very
near. When a sea-fog blots out the mainland for a
day, a feeling grows that the island may have slipped
anchor, and have drifted into unfamiliar seas. The
fisher-folk are not the only dwellers upon the islands ;
they are the home, the chosen resting-place, of ' the
Others,' the Fairies, the Fallen Angels, the mighty
Sidhe. From here they sweep across the sea,
invisible or taking at pleasure the form of a cloud, of
a full-rigged ship, of a company of policemen, of a
flock of gulls. Sometimes they only play with
mortals ; sometimes they help them. But often,
often, the fatal touch is given to the first-born child,

or to the young man in his strength, or the girl in her beauty, or the young mother in her pride ; and the call is heard to leave the familiar fireside life for the whirling, vain, unresting life of the irresistible host.

It is, perhaps, because of the very mistiness and dreaminess of their surroundings, the almost unearthly silences, the fantasy of story and of legend that lie about them, that the people of Aran and the Galway coast almost shrink from idealism in their fireside songs, and choose rather to dwell upon the slight incidents of daily life. It is in the songs of the greener plains that the depths of passion and heights of idealism have been reached.

It is at weddings that songs are most in use—even the saddest not being thought out of place ; and at the evening gathering in one cottage or another, while the pipe, lighted at the turf-fire, is passed from hand to hand. Here is one that is a great favourite, though very simple, and somewhat rugged in metre ; for it touches on the chief events of an islander's life—emigration, loss of life by sea, the land jealousy. It is called 'a sorrowful song that Bridget O'Malley made'; and she tells in it of her troubles at the Boston factory, of her lasting sorrow for her drowned brothers, and her as lasting anger against her sister's husband.

'Do you remember, neighbours, the day I left the white strand ? I did not find anyone to give me advice, or to tell me not to go. But with the help of God, as I have my health, and the help of the King of Grace, whichever State I will go to, I will never turn back again

'Do you remember, girls, that day long ago when I was sick, and when the priest said, and the doctor, that with care I would come through? I got up after; I went to work at the factory, until Sullivan wrote a letter that put me down a step.

'And Bab O'Donnell rose up and put a shawl about her. She went to the office till she got work for me to do; there was never a woman I was with that would not shake hands with me; now I am at work again, and no thanks to Sullivan.

'It is a great shame to look down on Ireland, and I think myself it is not right; for the potatoes are growing in the gardens there, and the women milking the cows. That is not the way in Boston, but you may earn it or leave it there; and if the man earns a dollar, the woman will be out drinking it.

'My curse on the curraghs, and my blessings on the boats; my curse on that hooker that did the treachery; for it was she snapped away my four brothers from me; the best they were that ever could be found. But what does Kelly care, so long as he himself is in their place?

'My grief on you, my brothers, that did not come again to land; I would have put a boarded coffin on you out of the hand of the carpenter; the young women of the village would have keened you, and your people and your friends; and is it not Bridget O'Malley you left miserable in the world?

'It is very lonely after Pat and Tom I am, and in great trouble for them, to say nothing of my fair-haired Martin that was drowned long ago; I have no sister, and I have no other brother, no mother; my father weak and bent down; and, O God, what wonder for him!

'My curse on my sister's husband; for it was he made the boat; my own curse again on himself and on his tribe. He married my sister on me, and he sent my brothers to death on me; and he came himself into the farm that belonged to my father and my mother!

A Connemara schoolmaster tells me: 'At Killery Bay one time, I went into a house where there was an old man that had just lost his son by drowning. And he was sitting over the fire with his head in his hands, making a lament. I remember one verse of it that said: "My curse on the man that made the boat, that he did not tell me there was death lurking in it." I asked afterwards what the meaning of that was, and they said there is a certain board in every boat that the maker gives three blows of his hammer on, after he is done making it. And he knows some-way by the sound of the blows if anyone will lose his life in that boat.' It is likely Bridget O'Malley had this idea in her mind when she made her lament.

Another little emigration song, very simple and charming, tells of the return of a brother from America. He finds his pretty brown sister, his 'cailin deas donn,' gathering rushes in a field, but she does not know him; and after they have exchanged words of greeting, he asks where her brother is, and she says 'beyond the sea'; then he asks if she would know him again, and she says she would surely; and he asks by what sign, and she tells of a mark on his white neck. When she finds it is her brother who is there and speaking to her, she cries out, 'Kill me on the moment,' meaning that she is ready to die with joy.

This is the lament of a woman whose bridegroom was drowned as he was rowing the priest home, on the wedding day :—

'I am widow and maid, and I very young; did you hear my great grief, that my treasure was drowned? If I had been in the boat that day, and my hand on the rope, my word to you, O'Reilly, it is I would have saved you sorrow.

' Do you remember the day the street was full of riders, and of priests and brothers, and all talking of the wedding feast ? The fiddle was there in the middle, and the harp answering to it ; and twelve mannerly women to bring my love to his bed.

' But you were of those three that went across to Kilcomin, ferrying Father Peter, who was three-and-eighty years old ; if you came back within a month itself, I would be well content ; but is it not a pity I to be lonely, and my first love in the waves ?

' I would not begrudge you, O'Reilly, to be kinsman to a king ; white bright courts around you, and you lying at your ease ; a quiet, well-learned lady to be settling out your pillow ; but it is a great thing you to die from me when I had given you my love entirely.

' It is no wonder a broken heart to be with your father and your mother ; the white-breasted mother that crooned you, and you a baby ; your wedded wife, O thousand treasures, that never set out your bed ; and the day you went to Trabawn, how well it failed you to come home.

' Your eyes are with the eels, and your lips with the crabs ; and your two white hands under the sharp rule of the salmon. Five pounds I would give to him that would find my true love. Ohone ! it is you are a sharp grief to young Mary ni-Curtain ! '

Some men and women who were drowned in the river Corrib, on their way to a fair at Galway, in the year 1820, have still their names kept green in a ballad :—

' Mary Ruane, that you would stand in a fair to look at, the best-dressed woman in the place ; John Cosgrave, the best a woman ever reared ; your mother thought that if a hundred were drowned, your swimming would take the

sway; but the boat went down, and when I got up early
on Friday, I heard the keening and the clapping of women's
hands, with the women that were drowsy and tired after the
night there, without doing anything but laying out the dead.'

There are laments for other things
A man taken up 'not for sheep-stealing or any crime,
but just for making a drop of *poteen*,' tells of his
hardships in Galway gaol.   A lover who has enlisted
because he cannot get the girl he loves—'a pity I not
to be going to Galway with my heart' besides death
arm'—tells of his hardships in the army : 'The first
day I enlisted I was well pleased and satisfied ; the
second day I was vexed and tormented ; and the
third day I would have given a pound if I had it to
get my pardon.'   And I have heard a song 'made by
a woman out of her wits, that lost her husband and
married again, and her three sons enlisted,' who
cannot forgive herself for having driven them from
home.   'If it was in Ballinakill I had your bones, I
would not be half so much tormented after you ; but
you to be standing in the army of the Gall, and
getting nothing after it but the bit in your mouth.'
Here is a song of daily life, in which a girl laments
the wandering and covetous appetite of her cow :—

'It is following after the white cow I spent last night ;
and, indeed, all I got by it was the bones of an old goose.
Do you hear me, Michael Taylor ?   Give word to your uncle
John that, unless he can lay his hand on her, Nancy will lose
her wits.
'It's what she is wanting, is the three islands of Aran for
herself; Brisbeg, that is in Maimen, and the glens of Maam

Cross; all round about Oughterard, and the hills that are
below it; John Blake's farm where she often does be bellow-
ing; and as far as Ballinamuca, where the long grass is
growing; and it's in the wood of Barna she'd want to spend
her life.

'And when I was sore with walking through the dark hours
of the night, it's the coastguard came crying after her, and
he maybe with a bit of her in his mouth.'

The little sarcastic hit at the coastguard, who may
himself have stolen the cow he joins in the search
for, is characteristic of Aran humour. The comic
song, as we know it, is unknown on the islands; the
nearest to it I have heard there is about the awkward
meeting of two suitors, a carpenter and a country lad,
at their sweetheart's house, and of the clever manage-
ment of her mother, who promised to give her to the
one who sang the best song, and how the country lad
won her.

Douglas Hyde, who is almost a folk-poet, the
people have taken so many of his songs to their
heart, has caught this sarcastic touch in this 'love'
song :—

'O sweet queen, to whom I gave my love; O dear queen,
the flower of fine women; listen to my keening, and look on my
case; as you are the woman I desire, free me from death.

'He speaks so humbly, humble entirely. Without mercy
or pity she looks on him with contempt. She puts mis-
pleading in her cold answer; there is a drop of poison in
every quiet word :—

'"O man, wanting sense, put from you your share of love; it
is bold you are entirely to say such a thing as that; you will
not get hate from me; you will not get love from me; you will
not get anything at all, good or bad, for ever."

' I was myself the same night at the house of drink; and I saw the man, and he under the table. Laid down by the strength of wine, and without a twist in him itself; it was she did that much with the talk of her mouth.'

There is another that I thought was meant to provoke laughter, the lament of a girl for her ' beautiful comb' that had been carried off by her lover, whom she had refused to marry, ' until we take a little more out of our youth,' and invites instead to ' come with me to Eochaill reaping the yellow harvest.' Then he steals the comb, and the mother gives her wise advice how to get it back :—

' He will go this road to-morrow, and let you welcome him; settle down a wooden chair in the middle of the house; snatch the hat from him, and do not give him any ease until you get back the beautiful comb that was high on the back of your head.'

But an Aran man has told me : ' No, this is a very serious song ; it was meant to praise the girl, and to tell what a loss she had in the comb.'

I am told that the song that makes most mirth in Aran is ' The Carrageen'; the day-dream of an old woman, too old to carry out her purpose, of all she will buy when she has gathered a harvest of the Carrageen moss, used by invalids :—

' If I had two oars and a little boat of my own, I would go pulling the Carrageen; I would dry it up in the sun; I would bring a load of it to Galway; it would go away in the train, to pay the rent to Robinson, and what is over would be my own.

' It is long I am hearing talk of the Carrageen, and I never knew what it was. If I spent the last spring-tide at it, and I to take care of myself, I would buy a gown and a long cloak and a wide little shawl; that, and a dress cap, with frills on every side like feathers.'

'(This is what the Calleac said, that was over a hundred years old :—)

' " I lost the last spring-tide with it, and I went into sharp danger. I did not know what the Carrageen was, or anything at all like it; but I will have tobacco from this out, if I lose the half of my fingers ! " '

This is a little song addressed by a fisherman to his little boat, his curragh-cin :—

'There goes my curragh-cin, it is she will get the prize ; she will be to-night in America, and back again with the tide. . . .
'I put pins of oak in her, and oars of red pine ; and I made her ready for sailing ; for she is the six-oared curragh-cin that never gave heed to the storm ; and it is she will be coming to land, when the sailing boats will be lost.
'There was a man came from England to buy my little boat from me; he offered me twenty guineas for her ; there were many looking on. If he would offer me as much again, and a guinea over and above, he would not get my curragh-cin till she goes out and kills the shark.'

For a shark will sometimes flounder into the fishing-nets and tear his way out; and even a whale is sometimes seen. I remember an Aran man beginning some story he was telling me with : ' I was going down that path one time, with the priest and a few others; for a whale had come ashore, and the jaw-bones of it were wanted, to make the piers of a gate.'

As for the love-songs of our coast and island people, they seem to be for the most part a little artificial in method, a little strained in metaphor, perhaps so giving rise to the Scotch Gaelic saying: 'as loveless as an Irishman.' Love of country, *tir-gradh*, is I think the real passion; and bound up with it are love of home, of family, love of God. Constancy and affection in marriage are the rule; yet marriage 'for love' is all but unknown; marriage is a matter of commonsense arrangement between the heads of families. As Mr. Yeats puts it, the countryman's 'dream has never been entangled by reality.' However this may be, my Aran friends tell me: 'The people do not care for love-songs; they would rather have any others.'

Yet I have just seen some love-songs, taken down the other day by a Kinvara man from a Connemara man, that have some charming lines :—

'Going over the hills after parting from the store of my heart, there is a mist on them and the darkness of night.'

'It is my sharp grief, my thousand treasures, my road not to be to the door of your house; it is with you I wore out my shoes from the beginning of my youth until now.'

'It is not sorry I would be if there was the length of a year in the day, and the leaves of the trees dropping honey; I myself on the side where the blossoms are falling, my love beside me, and a little green branch in her hand.'

'She goes by me like a little breeze of the wind.'

And this line that in a country of separations is already, they tell me, 'passing into a proverb':—

'It is far from one another our rising is every day.'

But the tradition of classical allusions, brought in some centuries ago, joined to the exaggeration that has been the breath of Irish poets, from the time Naoise called Deirdre 'a woman brighter than the sun,' has brought monotony into most of the love-songs.

The ideal country girl, with her dew-grey eye and long amber hair, is always likened to Venus, to Juno, to Deirdre. 'I think she is nine times nicer than Deirdre,' says Raftery, 'or I may say Helen, the affliction of the Greeks'; and he writes of another country girl, that she is 'beyond Venus, in spite of all Homer wrote on her appearance, and Cassandra also, and Io that bewitched Mars; beyond Minerva, and Juno, the king's wife'; and he wishes 'they might be brought face to face with her, that they might be confused':—

'She comes to me like a star through the mist; her hair is golden and goes down to her shoes; her breast is the colour of white sugar, or like bleached bone on the card-table; her neck is whiter than the froth of the flood, or the swan coming from swimming. . . . If France and Spain belonged to me, I'd give it up to be along with you.'

And he gives ' a thousand praises to God, that I didn't lose my wits on account of her.' Raftery puts distinction into each one of his songs ; but when lesser poets, echoing the voices of so many generations bring in the same goddesses, and the same exaggerations, and the same amber hair, monotony brings weariness at last.

There is an Aran song, ' Brigid na Casad,' that has more originality than is usual :—

' Brigid's kiss was sweeter than the whole of the waters of Lough Erne ; or the first wheaten flour, worked with fresh honey into dough ; there are streams of bees' honey on every part of the mountain, there is brown sugar thrown on all you take, Brigid, in your hand.

' It is not more likely for water to change than for the mind of a woman; and is it not a young man without courage will not run the chance nine times ? It's not nicer than you the swan is when he comes to the shore swimming; it's not nicer than you the thrush is, and he singing from tree to tree.'

And here is another, homely in the extreme in the beginning, and suddenly rising to wild exaggeration:—

' Late on the evening of last Monday, and it raining, I chanced to come into Seagan's and I sat down. It is there I saw her near me in the corner of the hearth ; and her laugh was better to me than to have her eyes down; her hair was shining like the wool of a sheep, and brighter than the swan swimming. It is then I asked who owned her, and it is with Frank Conneely she was.

' It is a good house belongs to Frank Conneely, the people say that do be going to it ; plenty of whiskey and punch going round, and food without stint for a man to get ; and it is what I think the girl is learned, for she has knowledge of books and of the pen, and a schoolmaster coming to teach her every day.

'The troop is on the sea, sailing eternally, and looking always, always on my Nora Ban. Is it not a great sin, she to be on a bare mountain, and not to be dressed in white silk, and the King of the French coming to the island for her, from France or from Germany?

'Is it not nice the jewel looked at the races and at the church in Barna? She took the sway there as far as the big town. Is she not the nice flower with the white breast, the comeliness of a woman? and the sun of summer pleased with her, shining on her at every side, and hundreds of men in love with her.

'It is I would like to run through the hills with her, and to go the roads with her; and it is I would put a cloak around my Nora Ban.'

The very *naïveté*, the simplicity of these ballads, make one feel that the peasants who make and sing them may be trembling on the edge of a great discovery; and that some day—perhaps very soon—one born among them will put their half-articulate, eternal sorrows and laments and yearnings into words that will be their expression for ever, as was done for the Hebrew people when the sorrow of exile was put into the hundred and thirty-seventh Psalm, and the sorrow of death into the lament for Saul and Jonathan, and the yearning of love into what was once known as 'the ballad of ballads,' the Song of Solomon.

I have one ballad at least to give, that shows, even in my prose translation, how near that day may be, if the language that holds the soul of our West Irish

people can be saved from the 'West Briton' de-
stroyer. There are some verses in it that attain to
the intensity of great poetry, though I think less by
the creation of one than by the selection of many
minds; the peasants who have sung or recited their
songs from one generation to another, having instinc-
tively sifted away by degrees what was trivial, and
kept only what was real, for it is in this way the
foundations of literature are laid. I first heard of this
ballad from the South; but when I showed it to an
Aran man, he said it was well known there, and that
his mother had often sung it to him when he was a
child. It is called 'The Grief of a Girl's Heart':—

'O Donall og, if you go across the sea, bring myself with
you and do not forget it; and you will have a sweetheart for
fair days and market days, and the daughter of the King of
Greece beside you at night.

'It is late last night the dog was speaking of you; the snipe
was speaking of you in her deep marsh. It is you are the
lonely bird through the woods; and that you may be without
a mate until you find me.

'You promised me, and you said a lie to me, that you
would be before me where the sheep are flocked; I gave a
whistle and three hundred cries to you, and I found nothing
there but a bleating lamb.

'You promised me a thing that was hard for you, a ship of
gold under a silver mast; twelve towns with a market in all of
them, and a fine white court by the side of the sea.

'You promised me a thing that is not possible, that you
would give me gloves of the skin of a fish; that you would
give me shoes of the skin of a bird; and a suit of the dearest
silk in Ireland.

'O Donall og, it is I would be better to you than a high,

proud, spendthrift lady: I would milk the cow; I would bring help to you; and if you were hard pressed, I would strike a blow for you,

'O, ochone, and it's not with hunger or with wanting food, or drink, or sleep, that I am growing thin, and my life is shortened; but it is the love of a young man has withered me away.

'It is early in the morning that I saw him coming, going along the road on the back of a horse; he did not come to me; he made nothing of me; and it is on my way home that I cried my fill.

'When I go by myself to the Well of Loneliness, I sit down and I go through my trouble; when I see the world and do not see my boy, he that has an amber shade in his hair.

'It was on that Sunday I gave my love to you; the Sunday that is last before Easter Sunday. And myself on my knees reading the Passion; and my two eyes giving love to you for ever.

'O, aya! my mother, give myself to him; and give him all that you have in the world; get out yourself to ask for alms, and do not come back and forward looking for me.

'My mother said to me not to be talking with you to-day, or to-morrow, or on the Sunday; it was a bad time she took for telling me that; it was shutting the door after the house was robbed.

'My heart is as black as the blackness of the sloe, or as the black coal that is on the smith's forge; or as the sole of a shoe left in white halls; it was you put that darkness over my life.

'You have taken the east from me; you have taken the west from me; you have taken what is before me and what is behind me; you have taken the moon, you have taken the sun from me; and my fear is great that you have taken God from me!'

1901.

JACOBITE BALLADS

I WAS looking the other day through a collection of poems, lately taken down from Irish-speaking country people for the *Oireactas*, the great yearly meeting of the Gaelic League; and a line in one of them seemed strange to me : '*Prebaim mo chroidhe le mo Stuart glegeal*,' 'my heart leaps up with my bright Stuart'; for I did not know there was still a memory of James and Charles among the people. The refrain of the poem was : 'Och, my grief, my friend stole away from me !' and these are some of its verses :—

'There are young girls through the whole country would sit alongside of me through a half-hour, till we would be telling you the story together of what it was put myself under trouble; I make my complaints, wanting my comrade. Och, my grief, my friend stole away from me !

'Where are my people that were wise and learned? Where is the troop readying their spears, that they do not smooth out this knot for me? Och, my grief, my friend stole away from me !

'I was for a while airy and beautiful, and all my treasure with my pleasant James. . . . On the top of all, my Stuart to leave me. Och, my grief, my friend stole away from me !

'It is the truth I cannot sleep in the night, fretting for my comrade; I to be lying down, and he weak under cold. My heart leaps up with my bright Stuart. Och, my grief, my friend stole away from me !

'It is hard for me to lie down after that; it is an empty thing to be crying the loss of my comrade, and I lying down with the mean people; it is my death the Stuart not to come at all. Och, my grief, my friend stole away from me!'

I had not heard any songs of this sort in Galway, and I remembered that our Connaught Raftery, whose poems are still teaching history, dealt very shortly with the Royal Stuarts. 'James,' he says, 'was the worst man for habits. . . . He laid chains on our bogs and mountains. . . . The father wasn't worse than the son Charles, that left sharp scourges on Ireland. When God and the people thought it time the story to be done, he lost his head. . . . The next James—sharp blame to him—gave his daughter to William as woman and wife; made the Irish English, and the English Irish, like wheat and oats in the month of harvest. And it was at Aughrim on a Monday many a son of Ireland found sorrow, without speaking of all that died.'

So I went to ask some of the wise old neighbours, who sit in wide chimney nooks by turf fires, and to whom I go to look for knowledge of many things, if they knew of any songs in praise of the Stuarts. But they were scornful. 'The Stuarts?' one said; 'no, indeed; they have no songs about them here in the West, whatever they may have in the South. Why would they, running away and leaving the country? And what good did they ever do it?' And another, who lives on the Clare border, said: 'I used to hear them singing "The White Cockade" through the country. "King James was beaten, and all his well-wishers; my grief, my boy that went with them!" But I don't think the people had ever much opinion of the Stuarts ; but in those days they were all prone to versify. But the famine did away with all that.' And then he also was scornful, and said : 'Sure, King James ran all the way from the Boyne to Dublin, after the battle. There was a lady walking in the street at Dublin when he got there ; and he told her the battle was lost ; and she said : " Faith you made good haste ; you made no delay on the road." So he said no more after that.'

And then he told me of the Battle of Aughrim, that is still such a terrible memory ; and how the 'Danes'—the De Danaan—the mysterious divine race that were conquered by the Gael, and who still hold an invisible kingdom —'were dancing in the raths around Aughrim the night after the battle. Their ancestors were driven out of Ireland before ; and they were glad when they saw those that had put them out put out themselves, and every one of them skivered.'

And another old man said : 'When I was a young chap knocking about in Connemara, I often heard songs about the Stuarts, and talk of them and of the blackbird coming over the water. But they found it hard to get over James making off after the Battle of the Boyne.' And another says of James : 'They liked him well before he ran ; they didn't like him after that.'

And when I looked through the lately gathered bundle of songs again, and through some old collections of Jacobite songs in Irish, I found they almost all belonged to Munster. And if they are still sung there, it is not, I think, for the sake of the kings, but for the sake of the poets who made them—Red-haired Owen O'Sullivan, potato-digger, harvestman, hedge-schoolmaster, whose poems are still the joy of the Munster people ; O'Rahilly, more learned, and as boundlessly redundant; O'Donnell, whose heart was set on translating Homer into Irish ; O'Heffernan, the blind wanderer ; and many others. For the Munstermen have always been more 'prone to versify' than their leaner neighbours on the bogs and stones of Connaught.

There is a common formula for most of these songs or 'Visions,' *Aislinghe*, as they are called. Just as artists of to-day find no monotony in drawing Ireland over and over again with her harp, her wolf-dog, and her round tower, so the Munster poets found no monotony in representing her as a beautiful woman, white-skinned, with curling hair, with cheeks in which ' the lily and the rose were fighting for mastery.' The poet asks her if she is Venus, or Helen, or Deirdre, and describes her beauty in torrents of alliterative adjectives. Then she makes her complaint against England, or her lament for her own sorrows or for the loss of her Stuart lover, spoken of sometimes as 'the bricklayer,' or 'the merchant's son.' The framework is artificial; but the laments are often very pathetic,

the love of Ireland, and the hatred of England born
of that love, finding expression in them.

John O'Donnell sees her 'like a young queen that
is going astray for the king being banished from her,
that had a right to come and set her loose.' O'Rahilly,
in one of his poems, shows the beautiful woman held
to her Saxon lover by some strange enchantment :—

'I met brightness of brightness upon the path of loneliness ;
plaiting of plaiting in every lock of her yellow hair. News of
news she gave me, and she as lonely as she was ; news of the
coming back of him that owns the tribute of the king.

'Folly of follies I to go so near to her ; slave I was made by
a slave that put me in hard bonds. She made away from me
then, and I following after her, till we came to a house of
houses made by Druid enchantments.

'They broke into mocking laughter, a troop of men of
enchantments, and a troop of young girls with smooth-plaited
hair. They put me up in chains ; they made no delay about
it ; and my love holding to her breast an awkward ugly clown.

'I told her then with the truest words I could tell her, it
was not right for her to be joined with a common clumsy
churl ; and the man that was three times fairer than the whole
race of the Scots, waiting till she would come to him to be his
beautiful bride.

'At the sound of my words her pride set her crying ; the
tears were running down over the kindling of her cheeks.
She sent a lad to bring me safe from the place I was in.
She is the brightness of brightness I met in the path of
loneliness.'

Sometimes the Stuart is almost forgotten in the
story of sorrows and the indictment of England.
O'Heffernan complains in one of his songs that many
of the heroes of Ireland have passed away, and their

names have never been put in a song by the poets ;
' and they even leave their verses without any account
of Charles the wanderer, though I promise you they
are not satisfied without giving some lines on
Seagan Buidhe' (one of the names for England).
Yet he himself, when very downhearted, 'on the edge
of the great wood under a harsh cloak of sorrow,' is
cheered by the pleasant sound of a swarm of bees
in search of their ruler ; and with the pleasant
thought that ' the harvest will be a bad one and with
no joy in it to Seagan. George will be sent back
over the sea, and the tribe that was so high up will
be left without gold or townlands ; and I not pitying
their sorrow.' And he winds up : ' In Shronehill, if I
were stretched at rest under a hard flag, and to hear
this story moving about so pleasantly, by force and
strength of my shoulders I would throw the sod off
me ; and I coming back leaping to hear the news.'

And another writer, Seagan Clarach, looks forward to seeing 'timid George tame upon the road,
without wine, without meat, without thread for his
shoes.' And his last verse, his ' binding,' is, ' I
beseech of God, I ask and I pray very hard, to cast
out the gluttons that tormented the generous race of
the Gael, from the island of the west, under hard
bonds, and to banish the foreign devils from us.'

For poets and people found it hard to forget
Cromwell ; and how ' the sons of the Gael are
scorched, tormented, pitchforked, put under the yoke,
by boors that are used to doing treachery.'

When the Stuarts come to mind, they are given fair words enough. 'The prince and heart-secret Charles that is sorrowful now and under weariness . . . will be under esteem ; and the Gael pleasant in the lime-white house.' . . . 'It is friendly, fair, bright, companionable, loving, brave, Charles will be, with sway, without a mist about him.'

And in one of Red Owen's 'Visions' he is told not to forget James, who is 'persevering, well-tempered, affectionate, stout, sweet, kind, poetical.'

Yet the Stuart seems to be always a faint and unreal image ; a saint by whose name a heavy oath is sworn. There are no personal touches such as I find in a song taken down from some country-man, on Patrick Sarsfield, the brave, handsome fighter, the descendant of Conall Cearnach, the man who, after the Boyne, offered to 'change kings and fight the battle again.' This ballad seems to have more of Connaught simplicity than of Munster luxuriance in it :—

'O Patrick Sarsfield, health be to you, since you went to France and your camps were loosened ; making your sighs along with the king, and you left poor Ireland and the Gael defeated—Och ochone !

'O Patrick Sarsfield, it is a man with God you are ; and blessed is the earth you ever walked on. The blessing of the bright sun and the moon upon you, since you took the day from the hands of King William—Och ochone !

'O Patrick Sarsfield, the prayer of every person with you ; my own prayer and the prayer of the Son of Mary with you, since you took the narrow ford going through Biorra, and since at Cuilenn O'Cuanac you won Limerick—Och ochone !

'I will go up on the mountain alone; and I will come hither from it again. It is there I saw the camp of the Gael, the poor troop thinned, not keeping with one another—Och ochone!

'My five hundred healths to you, halls of Limerick, and to the beautiful troop was in our company; it is bonfires we used to have and playing cards, and the word of God was often with us—Och ochone!

'There were many soldiers glad and happy that were going the way through seven weeks; but now they are stretched down in Aughrim—Och ochone!

'They put the first breaking on us at the Bridge of the Boyne; the second breaking on the Bridge of Slaney; the third breaking in Aughrim of O'Kelly; and O sweet Ireland, my five hundred healths to you—Och ochone!

'O'Kelly has manuring for his land, that is not sand or dung, but ready soldiers doing bravery with pikes, that were left in Aughrim stretched in ridges—Och ochone!

'Who is that beyond on the hill, Beinn Edair? I a poor soldier with King James. I was last year in arms and in dress, but this year I am asking alms—Och ochone!'

There are other symbolic songs besides the 'Visions.' Mangan's fine translation of Kathleen ni Houlihan is well known; and it is likely the king is calling to Ireland in '*Ceann dubh deelish*,' that is beautiful in all translations. This is *An Craoibhin's*:—

'The women of the village are in madness and trouble,
    Pulling their hair and letting it go with the wind ;
They will not take a boy of the men of the country
    Till they go into the rout with the boys of the king.

'Black head, darling, darling, darling,
    Black head, darling, move over to me ;
Black head brighter than swan and than seagull,
    It's a man without heart gives not love to thee.'

But most of the translations have been in the affected style of the early part of the last century, twisting the sense to give what was thought to be a romantic turn.   A verse of Seagan Clarach's, for instance, the lament of a farmer 'who has been wrestling with the world': 'The two that belong to me are without shelter, and my yoke of cattle without grass, without growth ; there is misery on my people, and their elbows without sound clothes,' is turned into :—

> ' The loved ones my life would have nourished
>   Are foodless, and bare, and cold.
>   My flocks by their fountain that flourished
>   Decay on the mountain wold.'

But there is one mistranslation for whose sake we must forgive many others, for it has given the sad refrain that has often been on Irish lips :—

> ' Seagan O'Dwyer a Gleanna,
>   We're worsted in the game ! '

Here are one or two of the many verses sung to the Little Black Rose by her lovers, poor or royal:—

' There is love through and through me for you all the length of a year; sore love, vexing love, lasting love, love that left me without health, without a road, without running ; and for ever, ever, without any sway at all over my Fair Black Rose.

' I would travel through Munster with you, and the boundaries of the hills, if I thought I could find your secret, or a part of your love.   O branch of the tree, it seems to me that you love me ; that the flower of kind women is my Fair Black Rose.'

'My heart leaps up with my bright Stuart!' James and Charles are, I think, the only English kings whose names, as it were by accident, have found their way into Irish song. And it is likely they are the last to find a place there, for the imagination of Ireland still tilts the beam to the national side ; and the loyalty the poets of many hundred years have called for, is loyalty to Kathleen ni Houlihan. 'Have they not given her their wills, and their hearts, and their dreams ? What have they left for any less noble Royalty ?

1902.

AN CRAOIBHIN'S POEMS

' "I WOULD much rather (and I take every occasion of making this protest) write, so to say, in a dead language and for a dead people, than write in those deaf and stammering (*sorde e mute*) tongues, French and English, notwithstanding they are the fashion with their rules and exercises." This is so with me. Alfieri wrote these words a hundred years ago, and they express what is in my own mind. I would like better to make even one good verse in the language in which I am now writing, than to make a whole book of verses in English. For if there should be any good found in my English verses, it would not go to the credit of my mother, Ireland, but of my stepmother, England.'

I have translated this from Douglas Hyde's preface to his little book of poems, lately published in Dublin, *Ubhla de'n Craoibh*, "Apples from the Branch." *An Craoibhin Aoibhin*, "The delightful little branch," is the name by which he is called all over Irish-speaking Ireland ; and a gold branch bearing golden apples is stamped on the cover of his book. The poems had already been published, one by one, in a weekly paper ; and a friend of mine tells

me he has heard them sung and repeated by country
people in many parts of Ireland—in Connemara, in
Donegal, in Galway, in Kerry, in the Islands of Aran.

Three or four of the thirty-three poems the book
holds are, so to speak, official, written for the Gaelic
League by its president ; and these, like most official
odes, are only for the moment. Some are ballads
dealing with the old subjects of Irish ballads—emigration, exile, defeat, and death ; for Douglas Hyde,
as may be guessed from his preface, has, no less than
his fellows—

> ' Hidden in his heart the flame out of the eyes
> Of Kathleen, the daughter of Houlihan.'

But these national ballads, though very popular,
are, I think, not so good as his more personal poems.
I suppose no narrative of what others have done or
felt or suffered can move one like a flash from ' that
little infinite, faltering, eternal flame that one calls
oneself.' Even in my bare prose translation, this
poem will, I think, be found to have as distinct a
quality as that of Villon or of Heine :—

> ' There are three fine devils eating my heart—
> They left me, my grief ! without a thing :
> Sickness wrought, and Love wrought,
> And an empty pocket, my ruin and my woe.
> Poverty left me without a shirt,
> Barefooted, barelegged, without any covering ;
> Sickness left me with my head weak
> And my body miserable, an ugly thing.
> Love left me like a coal upon the floor,
> Like a half-burned sod, that is never put out,

Worse than the cough, worse than the fever itself,
Worse than any curse at all under the sun,
Worse than the great poverty
Is the devil that is called " Love " by the people.
And if I were in my young youth again,
I would not take, or give, or ask for a kiss !'

The next, in the form of a little folk-song, expresses the thought of the idealist of all time, that makes him cry, as one of the oldest of the poets cried long ago, 'Mine heritage is unto me as a speckled bird ; the birds round about are against her.' Yet, with its whimsical fancies and exaggerations, it could hardly have been written in any but Irish air.

' It 's my grief that I am not a little white duck,
And I'd swim over the sea to France or to Spain ;
I would not stay in Ireland for one week only,
To be without eating, without drinking, without a full jug.

' Without a full jug, without eating, without drinking,
Without a feast to get, without wine, without meat,
Without high dances, without a big name, without music ;
There is hunger on me, and I astray this long time.

' It 's my grief that I am not an old crow ;
I would sit for awhile up on the old branch,
I could satisfy my hunger, and I not as I am,
With a grain of oats or a white potato.

' It 's my grief that I am not a red fox,
Leaping strong and swift on the mountains,
Eating cocks and hens without pity,
Taking ducks and geese as a conqueror.

' It 's my grief that I am not a fair salmon,
Going through the strong full water,
Catching the mayflies by my craft,
Swimming at my choice, and swimming with the stream.

' It's my grief that I am of the race of the poets ;
It would be better for me to be a high rock,
Or a stone or a tree or an herb or a flower
Or anything at all, but the thing that I am.'

The sympathy of the moods of nature with the
moods of man is a traditional heritage that has come
to us through the poets, from the old time when the
three great waves of the sea answered to a cry of
distress in Ireland, or when, as in Israel, the land
mourned and the herbs of every field withered, for
the wickedness of them that dwelt therein. The sea,
and the winds blowing from the sea, can never be
very far from the dweller in Ireland ; and they echo
the loneliness of the lonely listener.

' Cold, sharp lamentation
In the cold bitter winds
Ever blowing across the sky ;
Oh, there was loneliness with me !

' The loud sounding of the waves
Beating against the shore,
Their vast, rough, heavy outcry,
Oh, there was loneliness with me !

' The light sea-gulls in the air,
Crying sharply through the harbours,
The cries and screams of the birds
With my own heart ! Oh ! that was loneliness.

' The voice of the winds and the tide,
And the long battle of the mighty war ;
The sea, the earth, the skies, the blowing of the winds,
Oh ! there was loneliness in all of them together.

Here is a verse from another poem of loneliness:—

'It is dark the night is ; I do not see one star at all ;
And it is dark and heavy my thoughts are that are scattered
    and straying.
There is no sound about but of the birds going over my
    head—
The lapwing striking the air with long-drawn, weak blows,
And the plover, that comes like a bullet, cutting the night
    with its whistle ;
And I hear the wild geese higher again with their rough
    screech.
But I do not hear any other sound, it is that increases my
    grief—
Not one other cry but the cry and the call of the birds on the
    bog.'

Here is another, in which the storm outside and
the storm within answer to one another :—

' The heavy clouds are threatening,
    And it's little but they'll take the roof off the house ;
    The heavy thunder is answering
    To every flash of the yellow fire.
    I, by myself, within in my room,
    That is narrow, small, warm, am sitting ;
    I look at the surly skies,
    And I listen to the wind.

' I was light, airy, lively,
    On the young morning of yesterday ;
    But when the evening came,
    I was like a dead man !
    I have not one jot of hope
    But for a bed in the clay ;
    Death is the same as life to me
    From this out, from a word I heard yesterday.'

The next is very simple, and puts into more homely words the feeling of 'lonesomeness' that is looked upon as almost the worst of evils by the Irish countryman, as we see by his proverb: 'It is better to be quarreling than to be lonesome.' 'I would be lonesome in it,' is often the reason given for a refusal to go from bog or mountain cabin to some crowded place 'where there is not heed for one or love.'

'Oh! if there were in this world
    Any nice little place,
To be my own, my own for ever,
    My own only,
I would have great joy—great ease—
    Beyond what I have,
Without a place in the world where I can say:
    "This is my own."

It's a pity for a man to know,
    And it's a pain,
That there is no place in the world
    Where there is heed for him or love;
That there is not in the world for him
    A heart or a hand
To give help to him
    To the mering of the next world.

'It is hard and it is bitter,
    And a sharp grief,
It is woe and it is pity,
    To be by oneself.
It is nothing the way you are,
    To anyone at all.
It is nothing the way you are,
    To yourself at last!'

G

I suppose the following may be called a political
poem, from its elusive reference to Home Rule. I
was not sure on the point myself; for I thought the
wearer of the 'blue cloak and birds' feathers,' must be
a fine lady, perhaps laying enchantment on the fields.
But I heard some one ask the *Craoibhin* who he
meant, and his answer was: 'I suppose I was
thinking of an aide-de-camp':—

'I am looking at my cows walking,
  What are you that would put me out of my luck?
  Can I not walk, can I not walk, can I not walk in my own
    fields?

'I will not always be turned backwards.
  If there is need to be humble to you, great is my grief,
  If I cannot walk, if I cannot walk, if I cannot walk in my
    own fields.

'It's little my respect, and it's little my desire,
  For your blue cloak, and your birds' feathers.
  Can I not walk, can I not walk, can I not walk in my own
    fields?

'The day is coming as it's easy to see,
  When there shall not be among us the ugly like of you.
  And each one shall be walking, and each one shall be
    walking,
  Wherever shall be his will and his own desire.'

There are some love songs in the little volume.
But their writer has had, in his beautiful translations
of the 'Love Songs of Connacht,' to put such
intensity of passion into English, that he must
despair of putting any new wings to passion, or any
new exaggeration into lovers' words. In one of these

Connacht songs, the lover says : ' Blacker is the sun when setting than your features, Mary !' And she answers back : ' Neither star nor sun shows one-third as much light as your shadow !' Another lover says of the woman he desires : ' I will write largely of her, because of the thousands who hoped for her, and who have been lost ; and a hundred men of these who still live, are in pain and under locks through love. And I myself am not free, but am a bondsman in bonds.' And another boasts of ' a love without littleness, without weakness ; love from age till death, love from folly growing, love that shall send me close beneath the clay, love without a hope of the world, love without envy of fortune, love that left me outside in captivity, love of my heart beyond women.' Douglas Hyde's own love songs are quiet and staid in contrast to these ; but nevertheless they have a sober charm. Here are the last verses of one of them :—

' Will you be as hard,
    Colleen, as you are quiet ?
Will you be without pity
    On me for ever ?

' Listen to me, Noireen,
    Listen, aroon ;
Put healing on me
    From your quiet mouth.

' I am in the little road
    That is dark and narrow,
The little road that has led
    Thousands to sleep.'

In his preface to the ' Love Songs of Connacht,'
he says he finds in them ' more of grief and trouble,
more of melancholy and contrition of heart, than of
gaiety or hope '; and he writes : ' Not careless and
light-hearted alone is the Gaelic nature ; there is also
beneath the loudest mirth a melancholy spirit ; and
if they let on to be without heed for anything but
sport and revelry, there is nothing in it but letting
on.'   There is grief and trouble, as I have shown, in
many of his own songs, which the people have taken
to their hearts so quickly ; but there is also a touch
of hope, of glad belief that, in spite of heavy days of
change, all things are working for good at the last.

Here are some verses from a poem called ' There is
a Change coming' :—

' When that time comes it will come heavily ;
  He will grow fat that was lean ;
  He will grow lean that was fat,
  Without shelter for the head, without mirth, without help.

' The low will be raised up, says the poet ;
  The thing that was high will be thrown down again ;
  The world will be changed from end to end :
  When that time comes it will come heavily.

' If you yourself see this thing coming,
  And the country without luck, without law, without authority,
  Swept with the storm, without knowledge, without strength,
  Remember my words, and don't let your heart break.

' This life is like a tree ;
  The top green, branches soft, the bark smooth and shining ;
  But there is a little worm shut up in it
  Sucking at the sap all through the day.

' But from this old, cold, withered tree,
A new plant will grow up ;
The old world will die without pity,
But the young world will grow up on its grave.'

Here is a fine vision of a battle-field :—

' The time I think of the cause of Ireland
My heart is torn within me.

' The time I think of the death of the people
Who protected Ireland bravely and faithfully.

' They are stretched on the side of the mountain
Very low, one with another.

' Hidden under grass, or under tall herbs,
Far from friends or help or friendship.

' Not a child or a wife near them ;
Not a priest to be found there or a friar ;

' But the mountain eagle and the white eagle
Moving overhead across the skies.

' Without a defence against the sun in the daytime ;
Without a shelter against the skies at night.

' It's many a good soldier, joyful and pleasant,
That has had his laughing mouth closed there.

' There is many a young breast with a hole through it ;
The little black hole that is death to a man.

' There is many a brave man stripped there,
His body naked, without vest or shirt.

' The young man that was proud and beautiful yesterday,
When the woman he loved left a kiss on his mouth.

'There is many a married woman, with the child at her
     breast,
Without her comrade, without a father for her child to-
     night.

'There's many a castle without a lord, and many a lord
     without a house;
And little forsaken cabins with no one in them.

' I saw a fox leaving its den
Asking for a body to feed its hunger.

' There's a fierce wolf at Carrig O'Neill;
There is blood on his tongue and blood on his mouth.

' I saw them, and I heard the cries
Of kites and of black crows.

' Ochone! Is not the only Son of God angry;
Ochone! The red blood that was poured out yesterday!'

I do not know who the following poem was written
about, or if it is about anyone in particular; but one
line of it puts into words the emotion of many an
Irish 'felon.' 'It is with the people I was; it is not
with the law I was.' For the Irish crime, treason-
felony, is only looked on as a crime in the eyes of the
law, not in the eyes of the people :—

' I am lying in prison,
     I am in bonds;
To-morrow I will be hanged,
Who am to-night so quiet,
     So quiet;
Who am to-night so quiet.

' I am in prison,
 My heart is cold and heavy;
To-morrow I will be hanged,
And there is no help for me,
 My grief;
Och! there is no help for me.

' I am in prison,
 And I did no wrong;
I only did the work
Was just, was right, was good,
 I did,
Oh, I did the thing was good.

' It is with the people I was,
 It is not with the law I was;
But they took me in my sleep,
On the side of Cnoc-na-Feigh;
 And so
To-morrow they will hang me.'

' I am weak in my body,
 I am vexed in my heart,
And to-morrow I will be hanged;
Lying beneath the clay,
 My sorrow,
Lying beneath the clay.

' May God give pardon
 To my vexed, sorrowful soul;
May God give mercy
To me now and forever,
 Amen!
To me now and forever.'

But translation is poor work. Even if it gives
a glimpse of the heart of a poem, too much is

lost in losing the outward likeness.   Here are the
last lines of the lament of a felon's brother :—

> ' Now that you are stretched in the cold grave
>   May God set you free :
> It's vexed and sorry and pitiful are my thoughts ;
>   It's sorrowful I am to-day!'

I look at them and read them ; and wonder why,
when I first read them, their sound had hung about
me for days like a sobbing wind ; but when I look at
them in their own form, the sob is in them still :—

> Noıp ann ran uaıʒ ḟuaıp ó cá cu pínce
>   ʒo paopaıʒ Ɗıa ċu
> Iſ buaıɓeapċa, bpónaċ, boċc, acá mo ſmaoınce
> Iſ bponaċ mé anɓıú.

1900.

BOER BALLADS IN IRELAND

YESTERDAY I asked a woman on the Echtge hills, if any of her neighbours had gone to the war; She said : 'No ; but I know a great many that went to America when the war began—even boys that had business to do at home ; they were afraid of being brought away by the Press.' On another part of the Echtge hills, where a rumour had come that the police were to be sent to the war, an old woman said to a policeman I know : 'When you go out there, don't be killing the people of my religion.' He said : 'The Boers are not of your religion' ; but she said : 'They are ; I know they must be Catholics, or the English would not be against them.' Others on that wild range think that this is the beginning of the great war that will end in the final rout of the enemies of Ireland. Old prophecies say this war is to come at the meeting of these centuries ; and there is an old Irish verse which seems to allude to this, and which has been thus translated :—

'When the Lion shall lose its strength,
 And the bracket Thistle begin to pine,
The Harp shall sound sweet, sweet, at length,
 Between the eight and the nine.'

Lonely Echtge still keeps old prophecies and old
songs and some of the old speech, and but few newspapers are seen there ; but on the lowland, sympathy
with the Boers, and prophecies of their victory, are
put into the doggerel English verse that must be
poor in form, because a ballad, more than another
song, must have a long tradition of folk-thought and
folk-expression behind it ; and in Ireland this
tradition does not belong to the English language.
Even the beautiful air of 'The Wearing of the
Green' cannot give poetic charm to such verses as
these, which, like the others that follow, have been
sung and sold by ballad-singers in market-towns and
at fairs, and at country race-meetings, during the last
year :—

> 'Oh ! Paddy dear, and did ye hear
>   The news that 's going round ?
> No cheers for brave Paul Kruger
>   Must be heard on Irish ground.
> No more the English tourist at
>   Killarney will be seen,
> Unless you join the pirate's cause,
>   And chant " God save the Queen." '

Or this other, sung during the siege of Ladysmith :—

> 'And I met with White the General,
>   And he 's looking thin enough ;
> And he says the boys in Ladysmith
>   Are running short of stuff.
> Faith, the dishes need no washing,
>   Now they 're left so nice and clean ;
> Oh ! it 's anything but pleasant
>   To be starving for the Queen ! '

The defender of Ladysmith is treated with greater courtesy than some other generals, for, in spite of sympathy with the besiegers, the singer says :—

> ' But if he gave in to-morrow,
>   I would not think it right
> To throw the least disparagement
>   On a man like General White.
> He is making a bold resistance,
>   As great as could be made,
> Against their deadly Mauser rifles,
>   And their tremendous cannonade.'

The 'Song of the Transvaal Irish Brigade' has more literary quality :—

> ' The Cross swings low; the morn is near—
>   Now, comrades, fill up high ;
> The cannons' voice will ring out clear
>   When morning lights the sky.
> A toast we 'll drink together, boys,
>   Ere dawns the battle's grey,
> A toast to Ireland, dear old Ireland !
>   Ireland far away !
> Ireland far away ! Ireland far away !
>   Health to Ireland, strength to Ireland !
>   Ireland, boys, hurrah !

> ' Who told us that her cause was dead ?
>   Who bade us bend the knee ?
> The slaves ! Again she lifts her head—
>   Again she dares be free !
> With gun in hand, we take our stand,
>   For Ireland in the fray :
> We fight for Ireland, dear old Ireland !
>   Ireland far away !
> Ireland far away ! Ireland far away !
>   We fight for Ireland, die for Ireland—
>   Ireland, boys, hurrah !

> ' Oh, mother of the wounded breast !
> Oh, mother of the tears !
> The sons you loved, and trusted best,
> Have grasped their battle spears.
> From Shannon, Lagan, Liffey, Lee,
> On Afric's soil to-day,
> We strike for Ireland, brave old Ireland !
> Ireland far away !
> Ireland far away ! Ireland far away !
> We smite for Ireland, brave old Ireland !
> Ireland, boys, hurrah ! '

' The Irish Boy,' which is sung to the air of ' The Minstrel Boy,' is also in honour of the Irish Brigade :—

> ' While the Irish boy is on the shore,
> He 'll help to crush the stranger ;
> He 'll sweep them hence for evermore,
> And free thy land from danger.
> And then he 'll pray to God above,
> That his courage ne'er shall falter,
> To guard him to the land he loves—
> To Ireland o'er the water.'

Mayo is the county to which John MacBride, the leader of the Irish Brigade, belongs ; but I heard of a ballad-singer at Ballindereen, near my Galway home, the other day, whose refrain was :—

> ' And Erin watches from afar, with joy and hope and pride,
> Her sons who strike for liberty, led on by John MacBride ! '

At Galway Railway Station, whence the Connaught Rangers set out for the war, I have heard that wives, saying good-bye, begged their husbands ' not to be too hard on the Boers.' Anyhow, a 'Mother's lament for her son gone to the war,' that was sung at Galway Races the other day, shows more impartiality than most of the ballads :—

'When the battle rages fiercely, our boys are in the van ;
How I do wish the blows they struck were for dear Ireland!
But duty calls, they must obey, and fight against the Boer,
And many a cheerful Irish lad will fall to rise no more.

'I wish my boy was home again! Oh! how I'd welcome him,
With sorrow I'm heart-broken, my eyes are growing dim ;
The war is dark and cruel, but whoever wins the fight,
I pray to save my noble lad, and God defend the right!'

But it is the small farmers of Ireland who look with special sympathy on their fellows in the Transvaal. They give them a warning :—

'England sends her grabbers,
   From far across the sea,
To rob you of your friends and home,
   Likewise your liberty.'

And the Boers say in answer :—

'When we came to this country
   'Twas but a barren plain ;
But the honest hand of labour
   Was rewarded for its pain.
We found the precious metal,
   And of it we have great store ;
But Britain comes to rob us
   As she often done before.
      As she thought to do before,
      As she thought to do before ;
But Britain comes to rob us,
   As she often done before.'

Another ballad explains :—

' Those Boers can't be blamed, as you might understand ;
They are trying to free their own native land,
Where they toil night and day by the sweat of their brow,
Like the farmers in Ireland that follow the plough.
Farewell to Old Ireland, we are now going away,
To fight the brave Boers in South Africa ;
To fight those poor farmers we are not inclined :
God be with you, Old Ireland, we are leaving behind.'

Some verses—' The Boer's Prayer '—that I have
not seen on a ballad-sheet, but in a weekly paper,
give better expression to this feeling of farmer
sympathy :—

' My back is to the wall ;
    Lo ! here I stand.
O Lord, whate'er befall,
    I love this land !

' This land that I have tilled,
    This land is mine ;
Would, Lord, that Thou hadst willed,
    This heart were Thine !

' This land to us Thou gave
    In days of old ;
They seek to make a grave
    Or field of gold !

' To us, O Lord, Thy hand,
    Put forth to save !
Give us, O Lord, this land
    Or give a grave ! '

'A New Song for the Boers' says :—

> 'Hark! to the curses ringing
> From all smitten lands ;
> In sob and wail, they tell the tale
> Of England's blood-red hands.

> ' And wheresoe'er her standard flings
> Forth its folds of shame,
> A people's cries to heaven arise
> For vengeance on her name! '

But for passionate expression, one cannot, as I have already said, look to the comparatively new and artificial English ballad form ; one must go to the Irish, with its long tradition. Here is a poem, ' The Curse of the Boers on England,' which I have translated literally from the Irish :—

> ' O God, we call to Thee,
> This hour and this day,
> Look down on this England
> That has come down in our midst.

> ' O God, we call to Thee,
> This day and this hour,
> Look down on England,
> And her cold, cold heart

> ' It is she was a Queen,
> A Queen without sorrow ;
> But we will take from her,
> Quietly, her Crown.

> ' That Queen that was beautiful
> Will be tormented and darkened,
> For she will get her reward
> In that day, and her wage.

' Her wage for the blood
    She poured out on the streams ;
Blood of the white man,
    Blood of the black man.

' Her wage for those hearts
    That she broke in the end ;
Hearts of the white man,
    Hearts of the black man.

' Her wage for the bones
    That are whitening to-day ;
Bones of the white man,
    Bones of the black man.

' Her wage for the hunger
    That she put on foot ;
Her wage for the fever,
    That is an old tale with her.

' Her wage for the white villages
    She has left without men ;
Her wage for the brave men
    She has put to the sword.

' Her wage for the orphans
    She has left under pain ;
Her wage for the exiles
    She has spent with wandering.

' For the people of India
    (Pitiful is their case) ;
For the people of Africa
    She has put to death.

' For the people of Ireland,
    Nailed to the cross ;
Wage for each people
    Her hand has destroyed.

'Her wage for the thousands
　　She deceived and she broke ;
Her wage for the thousands
　　Finding death at this hour.

' O Lord, let there fall
　　Straight down on her head
The curse of the peoples
　　That have fallen with us.

' The curse of the mean,
　　And the curse of the small,
The curse of the weak,
　　And the curse of the low.

' The Lord does not listen
　　To the curse of the strong,
But He will listen
　　To sighs and to tears.

' He will always listen
　　To the crying of the poor,
And the crying of thousands
　　Is abroad to-night.

' That crying will rise up
　　To God that is above ;
It is not long till every curse
　　Comes to His ears.

' The crying will be put away ;
　　Tears will be put away,
When they come to God,
　　These prayers to His kingdom.

' He will make for England
　　Strong chains, very heavy;
He will pay her wages
　　With strong, heavy chains.

1901.

H

A SORROWFUL LAMENT FOR IRELAND

THE Irish poem I give this translation of was printed
in the *Revue Celtique* some years ago, and lately in
An Fior Clairseach na h-Eireann, where a note tells
us it was taken from a manuscript in the Gottingen
Library, and was written by an Irish priest, Shemus
Cartan, who had taken orders in France; but its date
is not given. I like it for its own beauty, and because
its writer does not, as so many Irish writers have
done, attribute the many griefs of Ireland only to
'the horsemen of the Gall,' but also to the faults and
shortcomings to which the people of a country broken
up by conquest are perhaps more liable than the people
of a country that has kept its own settled rule.

A SORROWFUL LAMENT FOR IRELAND.

My thoughts, alas! are without strength ;
My spirit is journeying towards death ;
My eyes are as a frozen sea ;
My tears my daily food ;
There is nothing in my life but only misery ;
My poor heart is torn,

And my thoughts are sharp wounds within me,
Mourning the miserable state of Ireland,
Without ease, without mirth for any person
That is born on the plains of Emer.
And here I give you the heavy story,
And the tale of all the remnant of her deeds.

She lost her pomp and her strength together
When her strong men were banished across the sea ;
Her churches are as holds of pain,
Without altars, without Mass, without bowing of
          knees ;
Stables for horses—this story is pitiful—
Or without a stone of their stones together.

Since the children of Israel were in Egypt
Under bondage, and scarcity along with that,
There was never written in a book or never seen
Hardship like the hardships in Ireland.
They parted from us the shepherds of the flock,
That is the flock that is astray and is wounded,
Left to be torn by wild dogs,
And no healing for it from the hand of anyone.
Unless God will look down on our distress,
Ireland will indeed be lost for ever !
Every old man, every strong man, every child,
Our young men and our well-dressed women,
Keening, complaining, and reproaching ;
Going under the power of the Gall or going across
          the sea.

                         H 2

Our dear country without any ears of corn,
Without store, without cattle, but only the green
    grass ;
Our fatherless children are wasted and weak,
Famine and sickness travelling over Ireland,
And every other scourge that was ever known,
And the rest of her pain has not yet been told.

   Nevertheless, my sharp woe ! I see with my eyes
That the High King has a bow ready in His hand,
And His quiver is full of arrows with sharp points,
And every arrow of them for our sore wounding,
From the sole of our feet to the top of our head,
To bruise our hearts and to tear our sinews ;
There is no spot of our limbs but is scarred ;
Misfortune has come upon us all together—
The poor and the rich, the weak and the strong ;
The great lord by whom hundreds were maintained ;
The powerful strong man, and the man that holds the
    plough ;
And the cross laid on the bare shoulder of every man.

   I do not know of anything under the sky
That is friendly or favourable to the Gael,
But only the sea that our need brings us to,
Or the wind that blows to the harbour
The ship that is bearing us away from Ireland ;
And there is reason that these are reconciled with us,
For we increase the sea with our tears,
And the wandering wind with our sighs.

We do not see heaven look kindly upon us ;
We do not see our complaint being listened to ;
Even the earth refuses us shelter
And the wood that gives protection to the birds ;
Every cliff, every cave, every mountain-top,
Every hill, every lough, and every meadow.

Our feasts are without any voice of priests,
And none at them but women lamenting,
Tearing their hair, with troubled minds,
Keening pitifully after the Fenians.
The pipes of our organs are broken ;
Our harps have lost their strings that were tuned
That might have made the great lamentations of
        Ireland ;
Until the strong men come back across the sea,
There is no help for us but bitter crying,
Screams, and beating of hands, and calling out.

It is not strength of hosts, not loss of food,
Not the horsemen of the Gall coming from Britain,
Nor want of power, nor want of calling to war,
That has put defeat upon the armies of Ireland,
And has filled the cities with a sad multitude,
Alas ! alas ! but the greatness of our sins.

See, we are now put in the crucible
In which every worthless metal is tried,
In which gold is cleansed from every tarnish ;
The Scripture is true in everything it says :

It says we must suffer before we can be cured ;
It is through repentance we shall find forgiveness,
And the restoring of all that we have lost.

   Let us put down the sum of our sins ;
Oppression of the poor, thieving, robbery,
Great vows held in light esteem ;
Giving our soul to the man that is the worst ;
The strength of our pride was greater than our life,
The strength of our debts was more than we could
       pay.

   It was with treachery Ireland was lost,
And the ill-will of men one to another.
There was no judge that would give a hearing
To the oppressed people whose life was under
       hardship.
Outcasts and widows crying aloud
Without right judgment to be had or punishment.

   We were never agreed together,
But as one ox bound and one free from the yoke ;
No right humility to be found.
All trying for the headship of Ireland
At the time when her enemies were doing their work.
No settlement to be made of any quarrel,
The share of the wheat-ear for the man that was
       strongest ;
It is long that this has been the hurt of Ireland ;
It is thus that the battle ended with the Gael.

A LAMENT FOR IRELAND

Let us turn now and change our manners,
Let us make repentance of our sins together—
It is thus that the Israelites came out of Egypt ;
Nineveh was given pardon for all its sins,
And even Peter for denying Christ.

O saints of Ireland, arise now together ;
O Patrick, who hast care of us, bless this flock :
We who are exiled, we who are forsaken,
This sod is gone out unless thou blow upon it ;
Is thy sleep heavy or is thy hearing slow
That thou dost not give an answer to us ?
Awake quickly; let it not be as a tale with thee
That there is no help for the fate of the Gael.

This, Patrick, is my own quarrel with thee
That every enemy of thy flock is saying
That thy ears are not ears that listen,
That thou art not troubled by the sight of thy people,
That if they did trouble thee thou wouldst not deny
    them.
Be with us nevertheless with thy strong power.
Make our enemies to quit Ireland for ever.

1900.

MOUNTAIN THEOLOGY

MARY GLYN lives under Slieve-nan-Or, the Golden
Mountain, where the last battle will be fought in the
last great war of the world; so that the sides of
Gortaveha, a lesser mountain, will stream with blood.
But she and her friends are not afraid of this; for an
old weaver from the north, who knew all things,
told them long ago that there is a place near
Turloughmore where war will never come, because
St. Columcill used to live there. So they will make
use of this knowledge, and seek a refuge there, if,
indeed, there is room enough for them all. There is
a river by her house that marks the boundary
between Galway and Clare; and there are stepping-
stones in the river, so that she can cross from Connaught to Munster when she has a mind. But she
cannot do her marketing when she has a mind; for
the nearest town, Gort, is ten miles away. The roof
of her little cabin is thatched with rushes, and a
garden of weeds grows on it, and the rain comes
through. But she is soon to have a new thatch; for
she thinks she won't live long, and she wouldn't like
the rain to be coming down on her when she is dead
and laid out. There is heather in blow on the hills

about her home, and foxglove reddens the clay-
banks, and loosetrife the marshy hollows ; and rush-
cotton waves its little white flags over the bogs.
Mary Glyn's neighbours come to see her sometimes,
when the sun is going down, and the hurry of the
day is over. Old Mr. Saggarton is one of them ; he
had his learning from a hedge-schoolmaster in the
old times ; and he looks down on the narrow teaching
of the National Schools ; and he was once in jail for
nine months, having been taken in the very act of
making *poteen*. And Mrs. Casey comes and looks at
the stepping-stones now and again, for she is a Clare
woman ; and though she has lived fifty years in
Connaught, she is not yet quite reconciled to it, and
would never have made it her home if she could have
seen it before she came. And some who do not live
among the bogs and the heather, but among the
green pastures and the grey stones of Aidne, come to
Slieve Echtge and learn unwritten truths from the
lips of Mary and her friends.

The duty of giving is taught as well as practised
by these poor hill-people. 'For,' says Mary Glyn,
' the best road to heaven is to be charitable to
the poor.' And old Mrs. Casey agrees, and says :
' There was a poor girl walking the road one night
with no place to stop ; and the Saviour met her on
the road, and He said : "Go up to the house you
see a light in ; there's a woman dead there, and
they'll let you in." So she went and she found the
woman laid out, and the husband and other people ;

but she worked harder than they all, and she stopped in the house after ; and after two quarters the man married her. And one day she was sitting outside the door, picking over a bag of wheat, and the Saviour came again, with the appearance of a poor man, and He asked her for a few grains of the wheat. And she said : "Wouldn't potatoes be good enough for you ? " and she called to the girl within to bring out a few potatoes. But He took nine grains of the wheat in His hand and went away ; and there wasn't a grain of wheat left in the bag, but all gone. So she ran after Him then to ask Him to forgive her ; and she overtook Him on the road, and she asked forgiveness. And He said : " Don't you remember the time you had no house to go to, and I met you on the road, and sent you to a house where you'd live in plenty ? and now you wouldn't give Me a few grains of wheat." And she said : "But why didn't You give me a heart that would like to divide it ? " That is how she came round on Him. And He said : " From this out, whenever you have plenty in your hands, divide it freely for My sake." '

And this is a marvel that might occur again at any time ; for Mary Glyn says further :—

'There was a woman I knew was very charitable to the poor ; and she'd give them the full of her apron of bread, or of potatoes or anything she had. And she was only lately married ; and one day, a poor woman came to the door with her children and she brought them to the fire, and warmed them, and gave them a drink of milk; and she sent out to the barn for a bag of potatoes for them. And the husband came in, and he said : " Kitty, if you go on this way, you won't leave much for ourselves." And she said : " He that gave us what we have, can give us more." And the next day when they went out to the barn, it was full of potatoes—more than were ever in it before. And when she was dying, and her children about her, the priest said to her : " Mrs. Gallagher, it's in heaven you'll be at 12 o'clock to-morrow." '

But when death comes, it is not enough to have been charitable ; and it is not right to touch the body or lay it out for a couple of hours ; for the soul should be given time to fight for itself, and to go up to judgment. And sometimes it is not willing to go ; for Mrs. Casey says :—

'The Saviour, one time, told St. Patrick to go and prepare a man that was going to die. And St. Patrick said : " I'd sooner not go; for I never yet saw the soul depart from the body." But then he went, and he prepared the man. And when he was lying there dead, he saw the soul go from the body; and three times it went to the door, and three times it came back and kissed the body. And St. Patrick asked the Saviour why it did that; and He said : " That soul was sorry to part from the body, because it had held it so clean and so honest." '

When the hill-people talk of ' the time of the war,' it is the war that once took place in heaven that is understood. And when '*Those*' are spoken of, the fallen angels are understood, the cloud of witnesses, the whirling invisible host; and it is only to a stranger that an explanation need be given.

'They were in heaven once,' Mary Glyn says, 'and heaven is the first place there was war ; and they were all to be done away with ; and it was St. Peter asked the Saviour to help them, when he saw Him going to empty the heavens. So He turned His hand like this; and the earth and the sky and the sea were full of them, and they are in every place, and you know that better than I do, because you read books. Resting they do be in the daytime, and going about at night. And their music is the finest you ever heard, like all the fifers, and all the instruments, and all the tunes of the world. I heard it sometimes myself, and there is no music in the world like it ; but not all can hear it. Round the hill it comes, and you going in at the door. And they are quiet neighbours if you treat them well. God bless them, and bring them all to heaven.'

And then, having mentioned Monday (a spell against unseen listeners), and said, ' God bless the hearers, and the place it is told in '—and her niece, Mary Irwin, having said, ' God bless all we see, and those we don't see,' they tell—first one speaking and then the other—that: 'One night there were *banabhs* in the house ; and there was a man coming to dig the potato-garden in the morning—and so late at night, Mary Glyn was making stirabout, and a cake to have ready for the breakfast of the *banabhs* and the man ; and Mary's brother Micky was asleep within on the bed. And there came the sound of the grandest music you ever heard from beyond the stream, and it stopped there. And Micky awoke in the bed, and was afraid, and said : " Shut up the door and quench the light," and so we did.' ' It 's likely,' Mary says, 'they wanted to come into the house, and they wouldn't when they saw me up and the lights about.' But one time when there were potatoes in the loft, Mary and her brothers were pelted with the potatoes when they sat down to supper. And Mary Irwin got a blow on the side of the face, from one of them, one night in the bed. ' And they have the hope of heaven, and God grant it to them.' ' And one day, there was a priest and his servant riding along the road, and there was a hurling of them going on in the field. And a man of them came out and stood in the road, and said to the priest : " Tell me this, for you know it, have we a chance of heaven ? " " You have not," said the priest. ("God forgive him," says Mary Irwin, " a priest to say that !") And the man that was of them said : " Put your fingers in your ears, till you have travelled two miles of the road ; for when I go back and tell what you are after telling me to the rest, the crying and the bawling and the roaring will be so great that, if you hear it, you 'll never hear a noise again in this world." So they put their fingers then in their ears ; but after a while the servant said to the priest : " Let me take out my fingers now." And the priest said : " Do not." And then the servant said again : " I think I might take one finger out." And the priest said : " Since you are so persevering, you may take it out." So he did, and the noise of the crying and the roaring and the bawling was so great, that he never had the use of that ear again.'

Old Mr. Saggarton confirms the story of the fall of the angels and their presence about us, but goes deeper into theology. 'The soul,' he says, 'was the breath of God, breathed into Adam, and it is the possession of God ever since. And I could never have believed there was so much power in the shadow of a soul, till I saw *them* one night hurling. They tempt us sometimes in dreams—may God forgive me for saying He would allow power to any to tempt to evil. And they would destroy the world but for the hope they have of being saved. Every Monday morning they think the day of judgment may be coming, and that they will see heaven.

'Half the world is with them. And when you see a blast of wind, and it comes sudden and carries the dust with it, you should say, " God bless them," and throw something after them. For how do you know but one of our own may be in it ?

'There never was a funeral they were not at, walking after the other people. And you can see them if you know the way—that is, to take a green rush and to twist it into a ring, and to look through it. But if you do, you'll never have a stim of sight in the eye again.'

(111)

HERB-HEALING

September 28th, 1899.

'HONOURABLE LADY GREGORY,

'I, Bridget Ruane, wish to inform you that there is in the Oratory in London one of the Fathers, a Saint. I do not know his name; but there was a young woman of the name of Meara; she got two falls and could get no cure. She went to London and found this holy man; and he sent her back to Gort, here to me, and I cured her. If your honourable Ladyship could make him out, it would be a wonderful thing, and a great happiness to many a weary heart, and the great God would have it in store for you and your son. May you enjoy many happy days together is the prayer of your humble servant,

'BRIDGET RUANE.'

This letter was brought to me one morning; and I went down to see the writer, a respectable-looking old woman, dressed in the red petticoat and blue cloak of the country-people. She repeated what she had said in her note, and added: 'Now if you could find out the name of that Saint through the press, he'd tell me his remedies; and between us, all the world would be cured. For I can't do all cures, though there are a great many I can do. I cured Michael Miscail when the doctor couldn't do it, and a woman in Gort that was paralyzed, and her two sons that were stretched. For I can bring back the dead with some of the herbs our Lord was brought back with, the *Garalus* and the *Slanlus*. But there are some things I can't do. I can't help anyone that has got a stroke from the Queen or the Fool of the Forth.

'It was my brother got the knowledge of cures from a book that was thrown down before him on the road. What language was it written in? What language would it be but Irish? May be it was God gave it to him, and may be it was the *other people*. He was a fine strong man ; and he weighed fifteen stone ; and he went to England, and there he cured all the world, so that the doctors had no way of living. So one time he got in a ship to go to America ; and the doctors had bad men engaged to shipwreck him out of the ship ; he wasn't drowned, but he was broken to pieces on the rocks, and the book was lost along with him. But he taught me a good deal out of it. So I know all herbs, and I do a good many cures ; and I have brought a good many children home to the world, and never lost one, or one of the women that bore them.'

I asked her to teach me some of her fragments of Druids' wisdom, the healing power of herbs. So she came another day, and brought some herbs, and sorted them out on a table, and said : 'This is

Dwareen (knapweed); and what you have to do with
this, is to put it down with other herbs, and with a
bit of threepenny sugar, and to boil it, and to drink
it, for pains in the bones ; and don't be afraid but it
will cure you. Sure the Lord put it in the world for
curing.

' And this is *Corn-corn* [tansy] ; it's very good for
the heart—boiled like the others.

' This is *Athair-talav*, the father of all herbs (wild
camomile). This is very hard to pull ; and when you
go for it, you must have a black-handled knife. And
whatever way the wind is when you begin to cut it,
if it changes while you 're cutting it, you 'll lose your
mind. And if you are paid for cutting it, you can do
it when you like ; but if not, *they* mightn't like it.
I knew a woman was cutting at one time, and a voice,
an enchanted voice, called out : " Don't cut that if
you are not paid, or you 'll be sorry." But if you put
a bit of this with every other herb you drink, you 'll
live for ever. My grandmother used to put a bit
with everything she took, and she lived to be over a
hundred.

' And this is *Camal buidhe* (loose-strife), that will
keep all bad things away.

' This is *Cuineal Muire* (mullein), the blessed candle
of our Lady.

' This is the *Fearaban* (water-buttercup) ; and it's
good for every bone of your body.

' This is *Dub-cosac* (trichomanes), that's good for
the heart ; very good for a sore heart.

I

'Here are the *Slanlus* (plantain) and the *Garblus* (dandelion); and these would cure the wide world; and it was these brought our Lord from the Cross, after the ruffians that were with the Jews did all the harm to Him. And not one could be got to pierce His heart till a dark man came; and he said: "Give me the spear and I 'll do it." And the blood that sprang out touched his eyes and they got their sight. And it was after that, His Mother and Mary and Joseph gathered these herbs and cured His wounds.

'These are the best of the herbs; but they are all good, and there isn't one among them but would cure seven diseases. I'm all the days of my life gathering them, and I know them all; but it isn't easy to make them out. Sunday afternoon is the best time to get them, and I was never interfered with. Seven Hail Marys I say when I'm gathering them; and I pray to our Lord, and to St. Joseph and St. Colman. And there may be *some* watching me; but they never meddled with me at all.'

A neighbour whom I asked about Bridget Ruane and her brother said:—'Some people call her "Biddy Early" (after a famous witch-doctor). She has done a good many cures. Her brother was *away* for a while, and it is from him she got her knowledge. I believe it's before sunrise she gathers the herbs; any way no one ever saw her gathering them. She has saved many a woman from being brought away when her child was born by whatever she does; and she told me herself that one night when she was going to the lodge gate to attend the woman there, three magpies came before her and began roaring into her mouth to try and drive her back.'

Another neighbour, who has herself some reputation as an herb-doctor, says :—' Monday is a good day for pulling herbs, or Tuesday—not Sunday : a Sunday cure is no cure. The *Cosac* is good for the heart. There was Mahon in Gort—one time his heart was wore to a silk thread, and it cured him. And the *Slanugad* (ribgrass) is very good : it will take away lumps. You must go down where it is growing on the scraws, and pull it with three pulls ; and mind would the wind change when you are pulling it, or your head will be gone. Warm it on the tongs when you bring it in, and put it on the lump. The *Lus-mor* is the only one that 's good to bring back children that are " *away*." '

Another authority says :—'Dandelion is good for the heart ; and when Father Quinn was curate here, he had it rooted up in all the fields about to drink it ; and see what a fine man he is. The wild parsnip (*Meacan-buidhe*) is good for the gravel; and for heart-beat there 's nothing so good as dandelion. There was a woman I knew used to boil it down ; and she 'd throw out what was left on the grass. And there was a fleet of turkeys about the house, and they used to be picking it up. At Christmas they killed one of them ; and when it was cut open, they found a new heart growing in it with the dint of the dandelion.'

But an old man says there are no such healers

now as there were in his youth :—' The best herb-doctor I ever knew was Connolly up at Kilbecanty. He knew every herb that grew in the earth. It is said he was away with the fairies one time ; and when I saw him he had the two thumbs turned in ; and it was said it was the sign they left on him. I had a lump on the thigh one time, and my father went to him, and he gave him an herb for it ; but he told him not to come into the house by the door the wind would be blowing in at. They thought it was the evil I had—that is given by *them* by a touch ; and that is why he said about the wind ; for if it was the evil there would be a worm in it, and if it smelled the herb that was brought in at the door, it might change to another place. I don't know what the herb was ; but I would have been dead if I had it on another hour—it burned so much—and I had to get the lump lanced after, for it wasn't the evil I had.

'Connolly cured many a one ; Jack Hall, that fell into a pot of water they were after boiling potatoes in, and had the skin scalded off him, and that Dr. Lynch could do nothing for, he cured. He boiled down herbs with a bit of lard, and after that was rubbed in three times, he was well.

'And Cahill that was deaf, he cured with the *Riv mar seala*, that herb in the potatoes that milk comes out of.'

Farrell says :—' The *Bainne bo blathan* (primrose) is good for the headache, if you put the leaves of it on your head. But as for the *Lus-mor*, it's best not

to have anything to do with that.' For the *Lus-mor*
is good to bring back children that are 'away,' and
belongs to the class of herbs consecrated to the uses
of magic, apart from any natural healing power.
The Druids are said to have taken their knowledge
of these properties from the magical teachers of the
Chaldeans; but anyhow the belief in them lives on
in Ireland and in other Celtic countries to this day.

A man from East Galway says : ' To bring anyone
back from being with the fairies, you should get the
leaves of the *Lus-mor*, and give them to him to drink.
And if he only got a little touch from them, and had
some complaint in him at the same time, that makes
him sick like, that will bring him back. But if he is
altogether in the fairies, then it won't bring him back,
for he'll know what it is, and he'll refuse to drink it.

'There was a man I know, Andy Hegarty, had a little
chap—a little *summach* of four years—and one day
Andy was away to sell a pig in the market at Mount
Bellew, and the mother was away some place with the
dinner for the men in the field; and the little chap was
in the house with the grandmother, and he sitting by
the fire. And he said to the grandmother: "Put down
a skillet of potatoes for me, and an egg." And she
said : "I will not; for what do you want with them?
you're just after eating." And he said : "Take care
but I'll throw you over the roof of that house." And
then he said : "Andy"—that was his father—"is after
selling the pig to a jobber, and the jobber has given
it back to him again; and he'll be at no loss by that,

for he 'll get a half-a-crown more at the end." So when the grandmother heard that, she wouldn't stop in the house with him, but ran out—and he only four years old. When the mother came back, and was told about it, she went out and got some of the leaves of the *Lus-mor*, and she brought them in and put them on the child ; and he went away, and their own child came back again. They didn't see him going, or the other coming ; but they knew it by him.'

And a Galway woman, who has been in England, says : ' I was delicate one time myself, and I lost my walk ; and one of the neighbours told my mother it wasn't myself that was there. But my mother said she 'd soon find that out ; for she 'd tell me she was going to get a herb that would cure me ; and if it was myself, I 'd want it ; but if it was another, I 'd be against it. So she came in and said she to me : " I'm going to Dangan to look for the *Lus-mor*, that will soon cure you." And from that day I gave her no peace till she 'd go to Dangan and get it ; so she knew I was all right. She told me all this afterwards.'

The man from East Galway says : ' The herbs they cure with, there's some that's natural, and you could pick them at all times of the day.'

' Sea-grass ' is sometimes useful as a natural and sometimes as an occult cure. One who has tried it and other herbs, says : ' Indeed the porter did me good, and good that I 'd hardly like to tell you, not to make a scandal. Did I drink too much of it ? Not at all. But this long time I am feeling a worm

in my side that is as big as an eel, and there's more of
them in it than that. And I was told to put sea-
grass to it; and I put it to the side the other day; and
whether it was that or the porter I don't know, but
there's some of them gone out of it.

' *Garblus*—how did you hear of that? That is the
herb for things that have to do with the fairies. And
when you crink it for anything of that sort, if it
doesn't cure you, it will kill you then and there. There
was a fine young man I used to know, and he got his
death on the head of a pig that came at himself and
another man at the gate of Ramore, and that never left
them, but was with them all the time, till they came to
a stream of water. And when he got home, he took to
his bed with a headache. And at last he was brought
a drink of the *Garblus*, and no sooner did he drink it
than he was dead. I remember him well.

' There is something in flax, for no priest would
anoint you without a bit of tow. And if a woman
that was carrying was to put a basket of green flax on
her back, the child would go from her; and if a mare
that was in foal had a load of flax on her, the foal
would go the same way.'

And a neighbour of hers confirms this, and says:
'There's something in green flax, I know; for my
mother often told me about one night she was spin-
ning flax before she was married, and she was up late.
And a man of the fairies came in—she had no right
to be sitting up so late: they don't like that—and he
told her it was time to go to bed; for he wanted to

kill her, and he couldn't touch her while she was handling the flax. And every time he'd tell her to go to bed, she'd give him some answer, and she'd go on pulling a thread of the flax, or mending a broken one ; for she was wise, and she knew that at the crowing of the cock he'd have to go. So at last the cock crowed, and she was safe, for the cock is blessed.'

Old Bridget Ruane will not do any more cures by charms or by simples, or 'bring children home to the world' any more. For she died last winter ; and we may be sure that among the green herbs that cover her grave, there are some that are 'good for every bone in the body,' and that are 'very good for a sore heart.'

1900.

THE WANDERING TRIBE

WHEN poor Paul Ruttledge made his great effort to escape from the doorsteps of law and order—from the world, the flesh, and the newspaper—and fell among tinkers, I looked with more interest than before at the little camps that one sees every now and then by the roadside for a few days or weeks. And I wondered why our country people—who are so kind to one another, and to tramps and beggars, that they seem to live by the rule of an old woman in a Galway sweet-shop: 'Refuse not any, for one may be the Christ'—speak of a visit of the tinkers as of frost in spring or blight in harvest. I asked why they were shunned as other wayfarers are not, and I was told of their strange customs and of their unbelief.

'They come mostly from the County Mayo,' I am told; 'and, indeed, they have not much religion; but last year Father Prendergast offered to marry a man and woman of them for nothing. But after he had them married, they made him give them a shilling for a lodging.

'The people wouldn't like to let them into their house; for if you would let one man in, maybe twelve families would follow them and take possession of the whole place.

'Some of them that do smiths' work are middling decent. They will sit there with their little pot and melt metal in it, and make things that belong to a plough ; but the most of them have no trade but to be going to fairs and doing tricks, and having a table for getting money out of you with games. Indeed the most of them are no better than pickpockets— " newks " they are called. And they never go to Mass ; and, as to marriage, some used to say they lepped the budget, but it's more likely they have no marriage at all.

'They never go in lodgings ; but they'll tilt up the cart, and put a bit of guano cloth over it and a little kennel of straw in it.   Or if a man is alone, he'll lay down on the sheltery side of a wall and sleep there. They are hardy with all the hardships they go through; they are the hardiest people in the world.

'And they make sport and fun sometimes.   I used to see them dancing at Rathin gate ; but no one would dance along with them; it is only among themselves they would have it.   And they sing songs too— " The sweet boy of Milltown " I heard them singing.

'There was a sweep in Gort joined them.   Charlie his name was.   He went into Greely's shop one time, that had set up a little public-house, and bid him give him five pounds and he'd make his fortune.   And he was afraid to refuse; and gave it to him, and off walked Charlie, and was never seen there again.

' He died after that in hospital. He slept out one night, and the frost went through his body. There was another of them stole two of old Quin's geese at Ballylee one night, and sold them to him again next day. After he had them bought, Mrs. Quin came down, and when she looked at them she knew them to be her own geese. " Give me back the money," she said. " I 'd be a fool if I did," said he, and he went away." '

Another neighbour says : ' They often made their camp in the boreen near my house ; but one of them never came into the house, and I never saw one of them at Mass. One very hard morning I passed by them as I was bringing in pigs to the fair of Gort. There they were, sleeping under an ass-cart, quite happy and satisfied. They fight at night and make friends again in the daytime ; and they sell their wives to one another ; I 've seen that myself.'

And an old man says : ' I think the tinkers are not the same as the rest of us ; I think they originated in themselves. They are very mirthful, and they have no control ; but sometimes there will be a tyrant among them that is a good fighter, and they will obey him.

' They have no religion ; and it might be true they don't believe in the devil—but what of that ? Aren't there many on your side and our own that think there is no resurrection, but that we go straight to heaven at the minute of death ?

' They never go into any house ; and there 's a great

many of them wouldn't go in a house if they were asked. My father went one time from Ballylee to Limerick ; and there was a tinker at that time the Government wanted to get information from ; something about Bonaparte it was. And they offered him a good lodging with a feather-bed in it to sleep on ; and he said if he slept one night on a feather-bed, he'd never be any good after ; that it was more wholesome to sleep outside on a bed of rushes. They didn't get any information out of him after ; though they offered him good reward, he wouldn't give it to them.

' They have no marriage at all ; but their women might be ten times better than the rural women for all that, and true to their men. The women are very smart at cooking. You'll see them make a fire by the roadside with a bundle of straw and a bit of wood, and they'll put the pot down. What goes into the pot ? Well, how would I know ? but the men are very handy, and when they put their hand in the pot, believe me it doesn't go in empty.

' They used to be prone to coining at one time ; but the law of transportation stopped that. And there's few of the police would like to grabble with them. I saw four of the police trying to take one the other day, and he bet them all ; and it was a countryman got a hold of him in the end.'

And a woman whose house they have often made their camp near, says : ' They are bad, and we don't like them to be coming near us. There was a little lad of them came running to the door one night, and he called to us to come ; for there was a man killing his mother. But we drove him away and didn't go ; for we knew her to be a bad woman.' And another woman says : ' If they have a religion, it 's a wandering one ; wandering like themselves.'

And a farmer living by the roadside says : ' A bad class they are, indeed, sleeping out under a little bit of cloth, and hardy for all that. Wild beasts they are, stealing turf from the banks.'

But an old man from Slieve Echtge takes a more kindly view of them. ' There are very nice men among them,' he says ; ' and they are as hardy as goats or as Connemara sheep. They go about to fairs and deal in asses and in horses, and sometimes they are rich. There was one I knew, a sieve-maker— they are of the same class—and that married a tinker's daughter ; they were in here two or three times. I told him I wondered they wouldn't settle down in one place ; for if I knew the way to make money, I said, I 'd make plenty—for they are said to coin money. But he said it made no difference if they had money ; they couldn't stop in one place ; they must be walking always and going through the whole country.'

And then we got to the reason of their wandering.

' It was a tinker put St. Patrick astray one time. For he was a slave in Ireland after he was brought out of France, and it would take a hundred pounds to buy his freedom. And he found a lump of gold or of

silver in a field one day, where he was minding sheep ;
and he brought it to a tinker and asked the value of
it. "It's nothing at all but a bit of solder," says the
tinker. "Give it here to me." But St. Patrick brought
it to a smith then, and he told him the value of it.
And then St. Patrick put a curse on the tinkers that
they might be for ever with every man's face against
them, and their face against every man ; and that
they should get no rest for ever but to travel the
world.

'And there are some say that when our Lord was
on the cross there could be no tradesman found to
drive the nails in His hands and His feet till a tinker
was brought, and he did it ; and that is why they have
to walk the world ; and I never met anyone that had
seen a tinker's funeral.

'But they may believe some things. For there was
a woman of them told me one time they were camping
near the railway bridge that in the night-time she
saw the whole wall beside her falling down and
shattered ; but in the morning it was standing as it
did before. "And we'll get out of this place as fast
as we can," she said.'

'They are a class of themselves,' says another man,
'and they have been there ever since the world began.
I often heard it said that our Lord asked a tinker one
time to make Him some vessel He wanted, and he
refused Him. He went then to a smith, and he did
what was wanted. And from that time the tinkers
have been wandering on the roads ; but they

wouldn't have refused Him if they had known He
was God.   I never saw them at Mass ; but I am sure
they believe in God.   It was here in Ireland they
refused our Lord, the time He walked the whole
world after the Crucifixion.'

'To be sure they are under a curse,' said another,
'like the Jews, to be wandering always ; and they
have some religion of their own, but it 's a bad one.
It 's likely St. Patrick put the curse on them ; for a
fleet of children of tinkers went after him one time,
mocking at him, and he turned one of them into a
pillar of stone.'

And that is their story as I have heard it so far.

WORKHOUSE DREAMS

LAST June I had a few free days, and I chose to
spend them among the imaginative class, the holders
of the traditions of Ireland, country people in thatched
houses, workers in fields and bogs.

I was looking for legends of those shadow-heroes,
Finn and his men, to help me in writing their story;
and I heard many tales and long poems about fair-
haired Finn, who 'had all the wisdom of a little
child'; and Conan of the sharp tongue, who was
'some way cross in himself,' and who had a briar on
his shield ; and their adventures beyond sea, and
their hunting after deer that were 'as joyful as the
leaves of a tree in summer time.' But some of the
people repeated verses by Raftery and Callinan and
Sweeny, and some told stories of the kingdom of
the Sidhe.

I spent three happy afternoons in a workhouse
in my own county, but not in my own parish ; and
after we had spoken of the Fianna for a while, the
old men began to tell me these long, rambling stories
I am about to repeat.

We sat in a gravelled yard, where only the leaves

of a few young sycamores told that spring had come. Some of the old men sat on a bench against the whitewashed wall of a shed, in their rough frieze clothes and round grey caps, and others stood round, pressing closer and closer as their interest in the story grew.

Some of the stories were new to me; some I had heard in other versions; but all—even those like the 'Taming of the Shrew,' which have, one must believe, been brought in from other countries—have taken an Irish colouring. I began to listen, half interested and half impatient; for I had never cared much for this particular kind of tale.

But as I listened, I was moved by the strange contrast between the poverty of the tellers and the splendours of the tales. These men who had failed in life, and were old and withered, or sickly, or crippled, had not laid up dreams of good houses and fields and sheep and cattle; for they had never possessed enough to think of the possession of more as a possibility. It seemed as if their lives had been so poor and rigid in circumstance that they did not fix their minds, as more prosperous people might do, on thoughts of customary pleasure. The stories that they love are of quite visionary things; of swans that turn into kings' daughters, and of castles with crowns over the doors, and lovers' flights on the backs of eagles, and music-loving water-witches, and journeys to the other world, and sleeps that last for seven hundred years.

K

I think it has always been to such poor people, with little of wealth or comfort to keep their thoughts bound to the things about them, that dreams and visions have been given. It is from a deep narrow well the stars can be seen at noonday · it was one left on a bare rocky island who saw the pearl gates and the golden streets that lead to the Tree of Life.

One of the old men told me a story in Irish— another translating it as he went on; for my ear was not practised enough to follow it well :—' There was a farmer one time had one son only, and the son died, and the father wouldn't go to the funeral, where he had had some dispute with him.

'And, after a while, a neighbour died, and he went to his funeral. And a while after that he was in the churchyard looking at the grave. And he took up a skull that was lying there—one of four—and he said: " It's a handsome man you may have been when you were young ; and I 'd like to know something about you," he said. And the skull spoke, and it is what it said : " I 'll go spend to-morrow night with you, if you 'll come and spend another night with me." " I will do that," said the farmer.

' And on the way home he met with the priest, and he told him what had happened. " I would never believe that a skull spoke," said the priest. " Come to my house to-morrow night, and you 'll hear him speak," said the farmer.

' So the next night they were sitting together in the house, and they had dinner set out on the table.

And after a while they heard something come to the door; and the skull came in, and it got up on the table, and it ate all the dinner that was there; and after that it went out again. "Why didn't you speak to it?" said the farmer to the priest. "Why didn't you speak to it yourself?" said the priest. "What will it do to me at all when I go to see it to-morrow night?" said the farmer; "but I must hold to my promise when it came here first."

'So the next evening he set out for the churchyard, and he could see nothing at all in it. And then he went down three steps that were beside the church; and presently he was in a field, and it full of men fighting one against the other with spades and reaping-hooks. "Is it looking for a head you are?" they said; "it's gone into that field beyond."

'So he went on into the other field; and it was full of men and women, all of them fighting one against the other. "Are you looking for a head?" they said; "it's after going into that field beyond."

'So he went into the third field; and there he saw a big house, and he went into it. And he saw a fire on the hearth, and a lady in the room, and a serving-girl. And the lady was walking up and down the room; and whenever she would go near to the fire to warm herself, the serving-girl would put her away from it.

'Then they said: "If it's for a head you're looking, it's within in the room."

'So he went into the room; and the head was there

K 2

before him, and it asked him would he have some
dinner; and he said he would, and it brought him
into a kitchen; and there were three women in it, and
the head bade one of them to give the man his
dinner; and what she put before him was a bit of
brown bread and a jug of water, and he did not think
it worth his while to eat that; and then the head
bade the second woman to give him his dinner, and
she gave him a worse dinner again; and then the
third woman was told to give it to him, and she spread
a nice table, and put the best of everything on it, and
he ate and drank; and then he asked the head what
was the meaning of all he saw.

'And the head said: "The men you saw in the first
field used to be fighting when they were in life, because
they had land near to one another, and they used to be
for moving the merings, and now they have to be fighting with one another for ever and always. And the
men and the women you saw, they were married
people that used to be fighting with one another, and
they must go on fighting for ever now. And the
lady you saw in the house, when she was in life, she
usedn't to let the serving-girl near to the fire when
she would come in wet and cold, and would want to
warm herself; and now the serving-girl is doing the
same to her, and that will go on to the Day of
Judgment.

'" And as to the three women in the kitchen," he
said, "those were my own three wives. And when I
asked the first wife for my dinner, she gave me

nothing but brown bread and a jug of water. And when I asked the second wife for my dinner, she gave me a worse dinner again. But the third wife when I asked her, set out a grand table, and a white cloth on it, and gave me the best of food and drink.

' " And as for yourself," he said, " the reason you were brought here is, that you wouldn't go to your son's funeral, because you had a falling out one day when you were ploughing the field together, but you went to a stranger's funeral. And go back now," he said, " to where your son was buried, and make your repentance there, and maybe you 'll get forgiveness at the last. And how long is it since you left your home ? " he said. " I left it on the afternoon of yesterday," said the farmer. " It is seven hundred years you are here," said the head. Isn't that a long time he was in it, and he thinking it was only a few hours ?

' So he went back to where his own son was buried ; and he knelt down there, and made his repentance, and asked forgiveness and his son's forgiveness. And at last a hand came up out of the grave and took his hand ; and then he and the son went up to heaven together.'

Another old man says : ' There was a Protestant and a Catholic one time ; and the Protestant said if the Catholic would come to his church one Sunday, he 'd go to his the next.

' So the Catholic went first to the Protestant

church for one day, and it seemed to him as if it was
a week he was in it.

'And the next Sunday the Protestant went into
the Catholic church ; and there he stopped for a year
and a day, and he thought it was only a few hours
he was in it.

'And at the end of that time he died, and he went
up before our Lord. And he had done some things
that were not good in his life, and our Lord said : " I
will give you as many years of heaven as there are
penfuls of water in the sea, and hell at the end of
that." " That is not enough of heaven," said the man.
Then our Lord said : " I will give you as many years
of heaven as there are grains in the sand, and hell
after that." " That is not enough of heaven," said the
man.   Then our Lord said : " I will give you as many
years of heaven as there are blades of grass on the
earth, and hell after that." " That is not enough of
heaven," said the man.   " And I will ask you for this,'
he said ; 'give me a year of hell for all these things
you have spoken of: the drops in the sea, and the
blades of grass, and the grains of the sand, and give
me heaven in the end."

'And when the Lord heard that, He said, " I will
give you heaven first and last."

'That is how the Catholic had him saved.'

Another old man says: 'There was a king one time
that had a daughter ; and she went out one day in the
garden, and there she saw a bird—a jackdaw it was—

and she thought it very nice, and she followed it on. And at last it spoke to her, and it said : "Will you give me your promise to marry me at the end of a year and a day?" "I will not," she said ; and she went into the house again.

'After that the king's younger daughter went out, and she saw the bird and followed it, and it asked her the same thing. And she gave her promise to marry it at the end of a year and a day.

'And at the end of that time a great coach and horses came up to the door of the king's house ; and the jackdaw came in, and he took the edge of the young girl's dress in his beak to draw her out of the house. And she went away in the carriage with him, and they came to a sort of a castle, and went into it. And there was no one in it ; but no sooner did they come in, than there was a table set out before them, with every sort of food and drink, and beautiful gold cups and everything grand. And when they had eaten enough, the bird said, "Don't be frightened at anything you may see ; and whatever happens, don't say one word ; for if you do, you will lose me for ever."

'And then some sort of people came in, and began hitting at the bird and attacking him, and he keeping out of their way. And at last they got to him, and began to knock feathers from him. And when the young girl saw that, she cried out, "Oh, they are destroying you, my poor jackdaw!" "Oh!" he said, "why did you say that? If you had not spoken," he said : " I would be all right; but now I must leave you for ever.   And here is a ring I will leave with you," he said : "and whatever desire you have, you will get it when you rub the ring."

'He went away then, and there was no one left in the house but the young girl ; and all was darkness around her.   And she went up the stairs ; and at last she saw a little sign of light through a hole in the roof; and she rubbed the ring, and she said : " I wish that hole to be made bigger."   And so it was on the moment, and more light came in.

'And then she wished she could be up on the roof, and so she was.   And from the roof she could see the sea, and there was a ship on it in the distance ; and she said : " I wish I could be on the deck of that vessel."   And there she was on the deck, and the sailors not knowing where did she come from.   And she said to the captain : "Can you give me something to eat?"   And he said : " That is what I cannot do, for the harness casks are empty, we are so long at sea ; and we have not as much meat in them as would go on the point of a knife."   So she rubbed the ring then; and there was a table before them, set out with every sort of food and drink, and they all had enough.

'And then they came to a strange country; and she said to the captain to leave her on land.   And she went up to a big house, where some great man lived, and she asked for employment as a sewing-maid. And they said : " You may sew one of those dresses that is for the master's daughter that is going to be married to-morrow. And mind you do it well," they said.

'So she brought away the dress to her room, and she wished it to be the best dress, and the best-sewed, that would be seen on the morrow. And when the morrow came, so it was.

'Then she went out into the garden, where there were beautiful flowers and trees ; and she fastened a thread of silk from one tree to another, to make a swing-swong, and she began swinging on it. And the young lady that was going to be married, came down the steps into the garden, and she wanted to go on the swing-swong. And the other said she had best not go on it where she was not used to it, and she might get a fall. But she said she would ; and the other warned her secondly not to go on it. But up she got, and the thread broke, and she fell and was killed on the spot.

'Then all the people came out; and when they saw her dead, they had a court-martial on the strange girl, and they were going to put her to death ; but she told them how it all happened. And when the jury heard it, they said there was no blame on her, where she had given two warnings.

'That's a closure now.'

'And what happened her after that ? '

'I don't know what happened her ; they let her off that time anyhow.'

'And what became of the bird?'

'How would I know? Didn't I say that's the closure?'

Then a young man said : 'I'll tell you a folk-tale :—

'It was in the good old time when Ireland was paved with penny loaves and the houses thatched with pancakes ; and there was a king had a son, and the mother died, and he married another wife; and she had three daughters, and their names were Catherine Snowflake, and Broad Bridget, and Mary Anne Bold-eyes, that had two eyes in the front of her head, and another eye in the back of her poll.

'And the stepmother got to be very wicked to the son then ; and she used to be giving everything to the daughters ; but he had nothing but hardship, and all they would give him to eat was stirabout.

'He was out on the fields one day with the cattle, and there was a little Black Bull there, and it said to him : "I know the way you are treated," it said, "and the sort of food they are giving you. And unscrew now my left horn," he said, "and take what you will find out of it."

'So the young man unscrewed the left horn ; and the first thing he took out was a napkin, and he spread it out on the grass ; and then he took out cups and plates, and every sort of food, and he sat down and ate and drank his fill. And then he put back the napkin and all into the horn again, and screwed it on.

'That was going on every day, and he used to be

throwing his stirabout away into the ash-bin; and the servants found it, and they told the queen that he was throwing away what they gave him, and getting fat all the same.

'The queen noticed then that he used to be going every day into the field with the cattle; and she bade her daughter, Catherine Snowflake, to go and to watch him there to see what would he be doing.

'But that day when he went up to the little Black Bull, it said: " Your step-sister will be coming to-day to watch you," he said: "and unscrew now my right horn, and take out a pin of slumber you will find under it, and when you see her coming, go and play with her for a bit, and then put the pin of slumber to her ear, and she will fall asleep." So he did as the Bull told him; and when he put the pin of slumber to Catherine Snowflake's ear, she fell into a deep sleep in the grass, and never woke till evening.

'The next day the queen sent Broad Bridget, that was a great big woman, to watch the step-brother; but the Bull warned him as before; and he put the pin of slumber to her ear, and she fell into a deep sleep, and saw nothing.

'The third day Mary Anne Bold-eyes was sent out, and the brother put her to sleep the same as he did the others. But if the two front eyes were shut, the eye at the back of her poll was open; and she saw all that happened, and she went back that evening and told her mother the way her step-brother got all he would want out of the Bull's horn.

'The queen sent out then and gathered all her fighting men together to kill the Bull. And they all
surrounded the field where the Bull was ; but there
were two or three hundred more cattle in it ; and the
Bull was running here and there between them, the
way they could not get near him. And at the end of
the second day he made for a gap and broke through
it, and came to where the queen was, and he took her
on his horns and tossed her as high as her own castle.
He called to Jack then ; and Jack put a halter on
him, and they rode away together where winds never
blew and the cocks never crew, and the old boy
himself never sounded his horn. And they overtook
the wind that was before them, and the wind that
was after them couldn't overtake them.

' They came then to a great wood, and the Black
Bull said to Jack : " Get up, now, into the highest tree
you can find, and stop there through the day, for I
have to fight with the Red Bull that is coming
against me. And unscrew my right horn," he said ;
" and take out the little bottle that is in it, and keep
it with you ; and if I am well at the end of the day,"
he said, " it will be white as it is now."

' The Red Bull came to meet him then, and his
head was as big as another's body would be ; and he
and the little Black Bull went to fight together ; and
Jack stopped up in the tree.

' And in the evening he looked at the little bottle ;
and what was in it was as white as before. So he
came down, and he found the Black Bull, and got up

on his back again ; and they went off the same as before.

'They came then to the wood where the White Bull was, and he came out to fight the Black ; and all happened the same as the first day.

'And Jack came down from his tree and got on his back again ; and they went on to another wood. And the Green Bull came to meet him this time ; and Jack went up in a tree. And at evening he looked at the little bottle, and it was red up to the cork.

'He got down then, and went to look for the little Black Bull, and he found him lying on the ground at the point of death ; and the Green Bull gave a great bellow, and made away and left him there.

'And the Black Bull said : "I am going from you now, Jack ; but I won't go without leaving you something," he said. "When I am dead, cut three strips of hide off me from the nape of the neck to the root of the tail, and put them about your body ; and they 'll give you the strength of six hundred men." '

Jack had many adventures after this ; he killed three giants, rescued a princess from a dragon, and married her. These were told with dramatic effect ; and the other men, young and old, who had gathered round the teller, cried out at each new splendid adventure : 'Good boy, Peter ; that 's it ; bring it out.' And the last words, telling how Jack and his Princess ' put on the kettle and made the tea,' were drowned in applause and laughter, and clapping of hands.

But I had already heard that part of the story, in almost the same words, in Gort Workhouse; and had given it to Mr. Yeats for his 'Celtic Twilight,' so I need not put it down here.

Then an old man said : ' There was a young man one time was out hunting ; and as he was going home, he heard the cry of a child beside a sand-pit. And he got off his horse to look what was it ; and it was a young little child was there, a girl. And he took her up on the horse and wrapped her up, and brought her home to his mother. And they reared her up, and she grew to be a beautiful young girl ; and the young man thought the world and all of her.

' But he got some sickness and died. And the mother was fretting for him always ; and she shut up his room and locked it, that no one could go in. And she did not like to be looking at the young girl, because of the son being so fond of her ; and she looked for a way to get rid of her.

' So she sent her out on a message into a wood that had wild beasts in it, and she thought they would make an end of her. And the girl went astray there, and lay down and slept for the night. And the beasts came and lay down beside her, and did her no harm at all. And there she was found in the morning, asleep among them.

' Then the mother thought of another way to get rid of her ; and she bade her to go to the son's grave and to spend the night there. So she went as she was told ; and she was crying on the grass. And then the young man came up out of it, and it is what he said : " My mother thought I would harm you if you came here, but I will not harm you ; I will help you. And take these three gray hairs from my head," he said, " and bring them back with you. And for every one of them my mother will have to grant you a request. And it is what you will ask her, to open my room that she has locked up for a day and a night. And at the end of a year, you will ask the same thing of her, and again at the end of another year."

' So the girl went back, and she asked to have the door opened, and she went in and stopped there for a day and a night. And at the end of the year she did the same, and again at the end of the third year.

' And after a while the mother said one day : " I wonder what she wanted in that room, and what she was doing in it." And she opened the door, and there she saw a fire on the hearth, and the girl sitting one side of it, and a child in her lap, and the son sitting the other side, and two children in his lap. For she had brought him back from the grave.

' And the son said : " What is wanting to me now is someone that will go and spend seven years in hell for my sake, to save my soul." " I will do that for you," said the mother. " It would be no use you going," he said. " I will do it," said the girl.

' So he said she might go ; and he gave a spoon that would give her drink, and a ring that would give her food, so long as she would keep them.

'So she went down to hell, and she stopped there seven years; and through all that time she got no rest, only on Sundays.

'And at the end of the seven years, she was going out, and she heard a voice saying: "Will you stop another seven years to save your father's soul?" "I will do that," she said. "Do not," they said; "for your father gave you no care, and did nothing for you." "No matter," she said; "I will give another seven years to save his soul."

'And at the end of the second seven years she was going out; and her mother, that had done nothing for her, asked her to stop another seven years for her soul; and she did that. And at the end of the twenty-one years, they gave her the three souls in a napkin, and she went out.

'And as she was going home, she met with an old man, and he said: "Give me what you have there." "Who are you?" "I am Almighty God," he said. "I will not give them to you," said the girl. And after a little time she met with another old man, and he said: "Give me what you have there." "Who are you?" she said. "I am Jesus Christ." "I will not give them to you;" and she went on. Then the third time she met with an old man, and he asked for what she had in the napkin. "Who are you?" she asked. "I am the King of Sunday." "Then I will give them to you," she said; "for in all the twenty-one years I went through, I got no rest at all but on the Sunday."

'She went home then; and at first they didn't know her, where she was so long away; and when the children came down to see her in the kitchen, they didn't know her.

'But when the man of the house knew she was in it, he went down and gave her a great welcome back to himself and the children again.'

Then another old man said : 'There was a king that used to make rules and to break rules, and that was very cunning ; and he wanted to get a good wife for his son. So he sent him out one day to look for a girl that he would fancy, and he brought one in. And the old king showed her a whole lot of gold and of treasures ; and he said : " What would you do if all this was yours? " " I would sit down and do nothing else but enjoy it," she said.

'So the king said to his son that she wouldn't suit, and that he should go look for another girl, rich or poor. So he brought in a poor girl ; and the king showed her the treasure, and he said : " What would you do if all this belonged to you ? " And she said : " Whenever I would take a sovereign out of it, I would try to put back two."

'So he said she would do, and that the son might marry her. But the girl said : " I will be well treated while you are in it ; but some day you might be gone, and my husband mightn't treat me so well. And make him give me his promise now," she said, " that if ever he turns me out of the house, I may

L

bring three ass-loads of whatever I myself will choose along with me." So he gave her his promise she might do that.

' Then the old king died; and the young one was, like himself, a law-maker and a law-breaker. And he thought a great deal of his own wisdom, and of the judgments he would give.

'Now, at that time there was a man had a mare that had a foal in a field; and in the field next it there was an old *garran*; and there was a little stream that made the mering between the two fields. And the foal took a habit of crossing over the stream to the other field where the *garran* was; and it got to be so friendly with him, and so fond of him, that at last it was hardly it would come back at all. And the man the other field belonged to laid a claim to it, where it was always in his ground.

' So the case was brought before the king; and he thought a long time, and at last he said to put the foal in a house that had two doors, one on each side, and to put the *garran* outside one door and the mare outside the other, and to see which would the foal follow. And they did that, and the foal followed the *garran*, and it was given to the owner.

'And the man it was taken from was vexed; and he went to the queen, and he told the injustice that was done to him. And she bade him to get a fishing-rod, and to go fishing in the river; and when the king would go by, to turn and to be fishing on the dry land.

'So he did that; and when the king was coming by, he turned and began fishing on the dry land. And the king stopped and asked why was he doing that. And the answer he gave was: " I think it no more foolish to be fishing on dry land than to believe that a foal would belong to a *garran*."

'When the king heard that, he guessed it was his own wife had given the answer to the man; and he went back and asked was it true she had put the man up to do what he had done. "It is true," she said. " Then you may clear out of this," he said, " and go back to your own place; for I won't keep a wife in the house that will be upsetting my judgments." "I must go if you bid me to," she said; "but do you remember your promise to me, to bring away three ass-loads with me of whatever I would choose?" "You may do that," he said. So she got the three asses, and on the first she put her clothes and some money. And on the second she put her two children. And then she came back to her husband and stooped down before him. " Get up on my back," she said, "till I put you on the ass, for it is yourself I choose to bring along with me for my third load. So long as I have you and the children with me, what do I care where I go?" " If that is so," said the king, " you may as well bring in your things again and stop with me. And I will never drive you away again," he said.'

Another man said: 'There was a man in Ballinasloe Asylum that was not very mad—just a little mad—and he used to be raking about the gate. And there was a clock over the gate ; and one day the doctor was going out, and he took his watch out and looked up, and he said to himself, " That clock is not right." "If it was right, it wouldn't be in here," said the man that was raking.'

' I have a sorrowful story,' says another man. ' I am blind, and I hurt my hip. And I have a brother fighting for the Queen and for the King, and a son fighting against the Boers, and neither of them ever sent me anything.' (But this was received without much sympathy, and with what I imagine to represent derisive cheers.)

A very wild-looking man told ' on behalf of a poor man inside'—to get him a bit of tobacco—a long story about a farmer who worked hard himself, to give his sons time for schooling.

' One of them made money in the West Indies by teaching, and he came back ; and his mother was in the house, and she didn't know him ; and he asked might he stop the night. " Indeed, I can't give you leave to do that," she said ; " for a travelling man stopped for a night not long ago ; and when he went away in the morning, he brought with him the flannel bawneen and the pants of the man of the house, that were hanging on the hedge to dry. But stop here for a while," she said, "and rest yourself."

' Presently the father came in, and didn't know him ; and when he heard what the wife had said, he was vexed, and said : "A thousand men might come the road, and not one of them do what that travelling man did. And I am sorry, sir," he said, "that my wife gave you such a reason."

'Then the potatoes were ready, and they were put on a skip for the dinner; and they asked the gentleman to help himself; and they gave him a knife, but it had but half a blade; and they said they were sorry to have no better a one to give him. But he peeled his potatoes with that.

'And then some one came in and asked would the young people come in and join a dance, for there was a piper in the next house. And the stranger asked to go with them. But at every dance-house there is a blackguard, and there was one there; and he began to mock at the strange gentleman. And one of his brothers that didn't know he was his brother, said to the blackguard : "It's a very mean thing of you to mock at a stranger." But he went on doing it.

'Then the stranger got up and went over to where his sister was, and slipped a letter into her apron that told who he was. And then he quenched the dip-candle over her, that was lighting the house, and he made for the man that mocked him, and gave him a blow that sent him into the hearth, and then he made away.

'And it was a long time before they could find the candle ; and when it was lighted, the man was found dead on the hearth. And the sister read the letter;

but she did not tell it was her own brother had come home.

'But after that he got a good place in the West Indies, and sent for them all there.'

Then an old man said : ' I was minding a man in the hospital one time, and he was lying quiet in the bed; and the priest came in to see him, Father Kearns.   And all of a sudden he made one leap, and was out of the bed, and bade the priest to be off out of that.   And the priest made for the door ; and I stood in the way of the man till he got out; and then I got out myself, and shut the door.   He was brought away to Ballinasloe Asylum after.   But if it wasn't for me, Father Kearns wouldn't have got safe out.

'That's my story.'

The first old man said : ' There was a man one time went to the market to sell a cow ; and he sold her, and he took a drop of drink after; and instead of going home, he went into a sort of a barn where there was straw stored, and he fell asleep there.

'And in the night some men came in, and he heard them talking.   And they had a lot of silver plate with them, they were after stealing from some house in the town, and they were hiding it in the straw till they would come and bring it away again.

'And he said nothing, and kept quiet till morning; and then he went out; and the people in the town were talking of nothing else but the great robbery of silver plate in the night. And no one knew who had done it; and the man came forward, and told them where the silver plate was, and who the men were that stole it; and the things were found, and the men convicted. But he did not let on how he had come to know it, or that he had slept in the barn.

'So he got a great name; and when he went home, his landlord heard of it; and he sent for him, and he said: "I am missing things this good while, and the last thing I lost was a diamond ring. Tell me who was it stole that," he said. "I can't tell you," said the man. "Well," said the landlord, "I will lock you up in a room for three days; and if you can't tell me by the end of that time who stole the ring, I'll put you to death."

'So he was locked up; and in the evening the butler brought him in his supper. And when he saw evening was come, he said: "There's one of them," meaning there was one of the three days gone.

'But the butler went down stairs in a great fright; for he was one of the servants that had stolen the ring, and he said to the others: "He knew me, and he said, 'There's one of them.' And I won't go near him again," he said; "but let one of you go."

'So the next evening the cook went up with the supper, and when she came in, he said the same way as before: "There's two of them," meaning there was another day gone. And the cook went down like the butler had gone, making sure he knew that she had a share in the robbery.

'The next day the third of the servants—that was the housemaid—brought him his supper; and he gave a great sigh, and said : "There's the third of them." So she went down and told the others ; and they agreed it was best to make a confession to him ; and they went and told him of their robberies ; and they brought him the diamond ring; and they asked him to try and screen them some way ; so he said he would do his best for them, and he said : "I see a big turkey-gobbler out in the yard ; and what you had best do is to open his mouth," he said, "and to force the ring down it."

'So they did that.   And then the landlord came up and asked could he tell him where the thief was to be found.   "Kill that turkey-gobbler in the yard,'' he said, "and see what can you find in him." So they killed the turkey-gobbler, and cut him open, and there they found the diamond ring.

'Then the landlord gave him great rewards, and everyone in the country heard of him.

'And a neighbouring gentleman that heard of him said to the landlord : "I'll make a bet with you that if you bring him to dinner at my house, he won't be able to tell what is under a cover on the table." So the landlord brought him ; and when he was brought in, they asked him what was in the dish with the cover ; and he thought he was done for, and he said : "The fox is caught at last." And what was under the cover but a fox ! So whatever name he had before, he got a three times greater name now.

'But another gentleman made the same bet with
the landlord; and when they came into the dinner,
there was a dish with a cover, and the man had no
notion what was under it; and he said: "Robin's done
this time"—his own name being Robin. And what
was there under the cover but a robin! So he got
great rewards after that, and he settled down and
lived happy ever after.'

Then a red-faced young man said : 'There was a
young man one time, and his name was Stepney
St. George, and his people said it was time for him to
get married ; and they brought twelve young ladies
to stop in the house, the way he would make a choice
among them. And he used to be talking with them
and walking in the garden; and there was one of
them he got to like better than the rest, and the
others got jealous of her, and used to be picking at
her. And when Stepney saw that, he brought her
out one day into a field where there was a bull, and
he covered with rings and bells of gold, and a golden
door in his side. And he opened the door and bade
her to go in there, where she would be safe from the
other eleven women.

'So she went in and he shut the door; and the
others did not know where was she gone, and they
were looking for her in every place. And they came
to where the bull was; and they began looking at him
and touching him, and just by chance one of them
touched a bell, and the door opened, and there was

the young lady inside. And they took her out, and brought her into the house; and she was sitting on the window-seat looking out at the river. And they pushed her over, and she fell into the water and was swept away.

'As to Stepney St. George, he was looking for her everywhere, but he could not find her. And one day he saw a poor travelling woman trying to cross the river, and she fell into it. And he thought it might be that way his own young lady was lost.

'And that put it in his mind to build a bridge across the river, and he got all the men that could be got, and they set to work. And they had a good bit of it made before night. But in the night all they had made of it was swept away. And the next day they were building again, and they sat up to watch it that night. But all the same it was all gone before morning, and they did not see anyone near it.

'The third night, Stepney St. George himself sat up to watch. And at last he saw a great black eagle, and it came flying towards the bridge; and, when it saw him, it called out : "What are you doing building this bridge to be in my way? I swept it away the last two nights, and I'll sweep it away again now." "If you do, I'll get satisfaction from you," said Stepney. "You will have to find me for that," she said. "And my name is Mother Longfield, and my house is at the other end of the world." And with that she went away; and Stepney followed everywhere looking for her; and at last he came to a house, and

an old witch came out, and she told him her name
was Mother Longfield. " And I 've got you here now
in my power," she said, " and you will have to do all
the work I will give you to do."

' So she brought him out then to a stable ; and she
gave him a fork, and bade him clear out all the dung
and litter that was in it. So he began the work ;
but for every forkful he would throw out, two
would come in its place, so that at last there was
no room for him in the stable, and he had to go
outside.

' A young girl came up to him then, and she asked
what was the matter. And he told her all that had
happened ; and she said, " I will help you." So she
took out a little fork, and she went into the stable ;
and it wasn't long before she had it sweet and clean,
that you could eat your dinner off the floor.

' He went back then to the house, and the witch
was at the door, and she asked how did he get on.
" Very well," he said. " I have the whole stable
cleaned out, sweet and clean." She looked very sharp
at him then ; and she said : " Take care did Lanka
Pera help you?" But he let on not to hear her,
and made no answer.

' The next day she gave him a hatchet that was as
blunt as a blunt knife ; and she told him there was a
forest he should cut down before night, or she would
make an end of him. So he went to the forest and
began to cut ; but as he cut, it grew thicker and thicker,
and the trees that were saplings in the morning were

large trees before afternoon. So when he saw there was no use going on, he stopped. And then he saw the young girl again, and she said : "I am come to help you." And she took out a small hatchet, and began to cut, and before long the whole forest was levelled down.

'He went back to the house whistling and singing ; and he told the witch he had cut down the forest, and she asked did Lanka Pera help him. But he said she did not—for she had told him not to let on he had seen her at all.

'The third day the witch showed him a hill a good way off, and a wild horse on it ; and she said what he had to do was to catch the horse, and if he did not do that, it was his last day to live.

'So he began hunting the horse, and trying to catch it ; but he could never get near it at all. Then the girl came to him, and she said : "You will never be able to catch it without my help. And I will turn myself into a mare," she said ; "and you can get on my back. But remember," she said, "not to put the spurs into me whatever may happen." She turned herself into a mare then, and he got on her back. And the old witch came out then and she called to Stepney : "Don't spare the spurs."

'They galloped off then after the wild horse, but they never could come up with it. And at last, in the heat of the race, Stepney forgot what the girl had said, and he pressed the spurs into the side of the mare till the blood came down.'

('Oh murder!' and a groan of pity from all the old men.)

'Then the mare fell, and the mare was gone; and it was the girl he saw before him, and her sides bleeding. And it is then he knew she was the young girl had been stolen from him at his own place after he shutting her up in the bull.

'She went then and called to the wild horse, and he came to her; and they both of them got up on him, and they went back to the witch's house. And when they got near it, the girl got up and turned herself into a mare again. And the witch came out to meet them, and she said : " I see you didn't spare the spur."

'And the witch said Stepney might have the girl if he could choose her out of thirteen. And he did that. And the witch wanted to keep her from him yet, but he wouldn't give her up; and he brought her to a house that was close by; and they made a plan to escape in the night; and they made the two horses ready to bring them away. And the girl made two cakes; and she left them with some of the servants, and she said : " The witch will be coming in to watch us for the night, and she will ask for a story; and stick a knife into one of the cakes when she asks that," she said.

'So they made off then by the back door; and the witch came to watch the house; and she said to the maid : " Tell me a story now while I 'm waiting." So she stuck a knife in one of the cakes, and it began to tell a story; and the witch sat there listening to it.

'And when it was done, she asked for another story; and the maid stuck a knife in another of the cakes, and it began to tell a story. And when that was done, the witch asked for another story, and the maid stuck a knife in the third cake, and it is what it said : "The two you think you are watching are off, and are on the way back to their own home."

'When the witch heard that, she took the shape of an eagle on her; and she flew out after them, and she came in sight of them. And they looked back, and saw her coming like a big black cloud in the air ; and the girl said to Stepney : "Take the bit of wood you'll find in the horse's ear, and throw it behind you." And he did that, and a great forest grew up behind them; and it is hardly the eagle could fly over it.

'Then they saw her coming again; and the girl said : "Take the drop of water you will find in the horse's other ear, and throw it down behind you." And when he did that, there was a great sea behind them ; and the eagle found it hard to pass it, but it did at last.

'And when she was coming up with them again, the girl took a bit of stone was in her own horse's ear, and threw it behind them. And a great mountain rose up, that kept back the eagle for a time. And then she took a brass ball out of the other ear, and she gave it to Stepney ; and bade him to throw it at a white mole that was on the eagle's breast. So he made a shot with it, and hit the eagle, and it fell dead there and then.

'Then the girl said to Stepney: "There is no danger now between us and home. But have a care," she said, "when you get home not to let a dog touch your face in any way, or you will forget me and all that has happened."

'So he said he would remember that. But when he got home and sat down in the house, his little lap-dog jumped up on him and licked his face. And on the moment he forgot all that had happened, and the girl he had brought home.

'And after a while he was going to be married to another lady, and all was ready for the wedding; and a poor-looking girl came to the door. And the servants bade her to go away, for the grand people in the house would not want her. "I think I have something would amuse them," she said. "I have a cock and a hen that can talk the same as living people."

'So when the company heard that, they sent for her; and she went up, and she put out the cock and the hen on the table, and she threw down a few grains of oats; and when the hen was going to pick at it, the cock drove her away. And the hen said then: "You should not do that, after the way I helped you, cleaning out the stable you were not able to clean by yourself." But Stepney took no notice of what she was saying.

' Then she threw a little more oats, and the cock was taking it all for himself. And the hen said again : " You should not do that, when you remember how I helped you to cut down the forest." But still Stepney took no notice of what was being said. Then she threw a little more oats, and the cock was shoving the hen away, and the hen said : " You would not have treated me this way the time I caught the horse for you, after you driving the spurs into my side."

' And with that Stepney remembered all ; and he jumped up, and drove all the others away, and took her for his wife, and they lived happy ever after.'

Another old man said : ' There was a mouse one time said to a robin, that they would lay up a store of provisions together against the winter. And he bade the robin to go up in the hedges and to be picking berries, and he would have the hole ready to put them in. And then he said : " Let you go to where they are threshing wheat ; for if they saw me there, they would kill me ; but if they see you, they 'll be throwing grains to you."

' So the robin went and brought back the grains ; and when the hole was full, the mouse said : " I have enough for myself now, and go and look after your own house-keeping for the winter."

' So the robin was vexed ; and they agreed to go fight it out. And when the day came, all the animals came together, and all the birds of the air. And the place they fought was in a field before a big house. And they fought till all were dead but one eagle.

' And the young man of the house came out and looked at the field ; and he saw the eagle moving, and it said to him : " Go in now, and bring me out three sheaves of wheat." So he did that ; and the eagle picked the grain off two of the sheaves, and then he was strong. And he said : " I will bring you now on a voyage if you will come with me. But go in first to the house and bring me out a bit of yellow soap." So he got the bit of soap ; and the eagle took him and the soap and the sheaf on its back, and flew away. And at last it began to get tired and to droop ; and the place where it dropped was in the middle of the sea. And the young man said : " I don't like this, to be left down into the sea." Then the eagle bade him to throw away the bit of yellow soap, and where he threw it there came a green island. And they rested on it, and eat the grain from the sheaf they had with them.

' Then the eagle took him up again ; and when they came to land, it threw him down. And there was a house near, and a giant came out of it ; and he brought him in, and said to his servant : " Give him barley bread to fatten him, and when he is fat enough, I will eat him." '

(Then he was given tasks to do, and a girl came to help him, much as Lanka Pera helped Stepney St. George in the other story.)

M

'And afterwards the girl said to him that they would make their escape; and they got into a boat; and what she brought with her was the three young pups of the dog that minded the giant's house.

'And when they had gone a little way on the sea, the giant missed them; and he sent the dog after them to bring the girl back. But as soon as the dog came close to them, and opened its mouth to take hold of her, she put one of the pups into it, and it turned back to the shore again to bring the pup safe to land. And the giant was very angry when he saw it coming without the girl, and he sent it after them again. And the girl did the same thing as before, and put the second pup into its mouth, that it turned back again. And the giant sent it back the third time, and gave it great abuse for coming to shore without her. And the third time she dropped the pup into the water, for she was vexed, the dog to come so often. And the dog would not pick it up at first, for he was afraid to pick it up again after all the abuse he got from the giant. But when he saw it going to drown, he took it up and turned back, and they were free of him then.

'And they came to land; and the young man left the girl down by a shoemaker's house while he went on to make all ready for her at his own house. But she bade him not to let a dog lick his face or touch it, or he would forget all about her. But when he went in, his dog jumped up and licked his face; and he forgot the girl or that he ever had seen her.

' And as for her, she waited ; and he did not come back, and she knew no one in the place; and she went up in a tree that was over the well in the shoemaker's garden to hide herself. And after a while the shoemaker sent out one of his daughters to the well to bring in water. And when she stooped down, she saw the shadow of the girl in the tree, and she thought it was herself, and she said : " My father should not be sending such a handsome girl as that to be bringing in water ; " and she threw the tin can down against a wall and broke it, and went in.

' Then the shoemaker sent out the second daughter for water; and she stooped down ; and she thought it was her own face she saw ; and she no better-looking than myself, and that 's not saying much.' (Applause from all the old men.) ' So she wouldn't bring the water, but went in without it.

' Then he sent his missus out, that was the ugliest you ever saw—old and withered. But that did not hinder her from thinking the shadow she saw was herself ; and it is proud she was going into the house again.

' So at last the shoemaker himself went out, and when he stooped and saw the shadow, he looked up in the tree, and he said: " Come down out of that, for you have given me trouble enough." So she came down, and told him her story ; and he brought her to the young man's house.' (The cock and hen now come in as in Lanka Pera.) ' And they lived happily ever after.'

Another says : 'There was a young man killed a
deer one time he was out hunting. And a lion and
a hound and a hawk came by, and they asked a
share of it. And he gave the flesh to the lion, and
the bones to the dog, and the guts to the hawk.
And they thanked him ; and they said from that time
he would have the strength of a lion, and the quick-
ness of a hound, and the lightness of a hawk.

'It was a good while after that he fell in love with a
young girl; and her father said that before he could
marry her he must go out and see who was it was
stealing his cows ; for there were some of them stolen
every night.

'So he watched, and he saw a witch coming and
driving them away. And he attacked her, and fought
with her, and beat her by his strength, and she made
off. And he went to the place she had driven the
cows, that was underground, and he found the cows
belonging to the whole neighbourhood. And he
drove them all out, and gave them to the owners.

'And after a little time the father said to him, that
there was a fox in the country, that no hound could
catch, and that it was to be hunted again on the next
day. So the young man went out, and when he saw
the fox, he took the shape of a hound and followed
it. And he was gaining on it, and it took to a lake,
and he went in after it, and it turned to its own shape
of a witch, and dragged him down.

'The girl used to go and be looking at the lake
every day, but she never got a sight of him. And at

last, someone told her those water-witches were very fond of music, and to get a musical instrument. So she brought a musical instrument to the side of the lake, and she was playing it; and the witch put up her hand out of the water. "What will you take for that?" she said. "I will give it to you," the girl said, "if you will let me see my husband's head above the water." "I will do that much for you," said the witch.

'Then the young man put up his head above the water, and she could see his face; but she could not touch him, and she went away.

'The next day she came again with a musical instrument that was better again than the first, and she began to play it. The witch put up her hand, and asked what would she take for it. "Let me see my husband to his waist this time," she said. So the young man was let up out of the water as far as his waist, and then he disappeared again.

'The next day she came again, and the musical instrument she brought with her was seven times better than the other two. "What will you take for that?" said the witch. "Let my husband stand up on your shoulders, clear and clean out of the water," she said. So the witch put him up on her shoulder; and when she did, he took the shape of a hawk on the moment, and away with him through the air, back to his own home again.

'The witch followed him then; and when he was in a field, she came to fight him, and they fought the whole day, and they were both tired, and they stopped to rest. "Oh, if I had three drops of sea-water and a crumb of wheaten bread!" said the witch. "Oh, if I had three drops of fresh water and a crumb of barley bread!" said the young man.

'And a fairy brought the witch the three drops of sea-water and the crumb of bread. And a little serving-girl from the farm brought the young man the three drops of fresh water and the crumb of bread. And then they fought together again; and he having the strength of a lion, he killed her in the end.'

Another old man said: 'There was a young man looking for service one time; and a farmer said he would take him to mind his cattle. For a great many of his cattle had died with the herds he had, and he didn't know what the reason was.

'So the first morning the young man led them up as he was told, to the green grassy place on the top of Cruachmaa. And when he looked about him there, he noticed it to be very dirty and trampled by the cattle. So he brought them to graze in the fields at the side of the hill; and he came back, and cleared all the dirt from that field till it was green and smooth. And no more of the cattle died.

'He was up in the field one day, and he saw a great hurling match going on; and one side had a young man at the head of it, and it was beating the other. So the next day he went to the wood, and he cut a hurl; and he was all that day and the next shaping it; and his mother asked was he going to a match, and he said he was only amusing himself with it.

'The next night he went up to the field to give a hand; and the king of the fairies came up to him, and asked would he join his side that was the weakest, and he said he would. And he drove the ball to the goal every time, and they gave the other side a great beating. And the king of the fairies thanked him, and said they had been able to do nothing till they had a living person along with them.

'Then the king asked would he come along with him to bring away the King of Spain's daughter that he wanted for a wife. And the young man agreed to that. And the king raised them both into the air as if they were a wisp of straw; and they flew away on the air like two feathers.

'When they came to the court of the King of Spain, there was a great ball going on; and they went in, but no one could see them. And the fairy king said to the young man that he would know which was the princess by hearing her sneeze. And presently the most beautiful young lady that was there gave a sneeze; and the young man said, " God bless her." " Don't say that again," said the fairy king, " or she 'll be lost to us." So she sneezed twice after that, and he said nothing. And then the fairy king said: " Let you take hold of her now and bring her out, and I will make something in her own shape to put in her place, the way they won't miss her." So the

young man took a hold of her and brought her outside ; and then the fairy king came out, and they went
away like feathers in the air.

'And when they came to Irish land, the fairy king
said : "Now you may give her to me." "Indeed I
will not," said the young man, "after all the trouble
I went through ; but I will keep her for myself to be
my own wife." "If you do," said the fairy king,
"you will have nothing better than a stone, for she
will have no speech."

'But the young man brought her to his own house;
and his mother seeing her in her ball dress, thought
it was one of the ladies from Castle Hacket come for
a visit, and she was astonished when the son said she
was to be his wife. But all the time she could not
speak ; and at last the young man went up to the
field on the hill, and he brought a tar-barrel with him,
and he gathered sticks and ferns, and put them all
around, and began to set fire to them.

'Then the fairy king came and asked what was he
doing. "I am burning you out of the place," he said,
"till you give back speech to my wife." So the king
agreed to that, and they made friends again ; and the
young man went home, and found his wife speaking.
And she wrote a letter then to her father and mother,
the King and Queen of Spain ; and they were very
glad to hear that she was well, and they sent her
money and clothes of all sorts.

'Then the fairy king came and asked the young
man to go with him to Germany to help him to bring

back a wife for himself from the king's court there. So he agreed to go ; and before he went, the wife said : " When you come back, you will bring a title for yourself, and put an O to your name. And it is what you must do," she said, " when you are near the land, cut off your hand, and throw it on the shore, and bring it back to me after."

'So they went to Germany, and brought away a wife for the fairy king. And when they were coming home and were near the strand, the young man cut off his hand, and threw it on the land.

' And his wife put the hand on to him again after ; and he was O'Connor from that time, that was the first of all ; and the fairy king put an O to his name, and he was O'Neill, that was second.

' But now at this time, there isn't a Tom, Dick, or John, but puts an O before his name.'

An old one-eyed man gave me a new version of Deirdre's story. He said : ' The King of Ulster and his men were out hunting one time; and they met with the fairy king, Mannanan of the Hill. They sat down with him ; and himself and the King of Ulster began to play cards together, and whichever of them won could put some command upon the other. It was Mannanan won ; and what he put on the King of Ulster was to follow after him to whatever place he would go.

' With that he changed into the shape of a hare, and away with him, and the hounds after him, and

the king and his men after them again ; but they lost
sight of him. But the hounds followed on till they
came to a hill, and an old stump of a tree on top of it;
and they began scratching at the stump where it was
rotten. And when there was a hole scratched in it,
the king looked down; and he saw steps; and he and
his men went down the steps ; and they passed
through gardens and beside a pond with flowers
about it; and then they came to a big house, and in it
an old man sitting on a chair reading a book; and
they knew him to be Mannanan that they were
looking for.

'And he rose up and bade them welcome ; and there
was a feast spread out before them, with every sort of
food and drink. And while they were at the feast
they heard something like the cry of a child from an
inner room. And the King of Ulster rose up, and he
said : " I will go see what is in there ; for that is the
cry of a child."

' So he went in ; and he came back again, bringing
a baby in his arms, the most beautiful that was ever
seen, and her hair like gold. " I will bring away this
child with me, and rear her up," he said. " Do not,"
said Mannanan; "for if you do, your country will be
destroyed, and your throne will be lost through her,
and there will be a great many killed for her sake."

' But the king would not mind him; but he brought
her away, and he had a house made for her, and she
was reared up in it. And she grew to be a nice
young girl, and there were women about her to care

her and to attend on her; but she never saw a man but the king himself, that used to come and see her every week. And he had great love for her; and he thought she loved him.'

The account of Deirdre's meeting with Naoise, and their flight to Scotland, and the king's message bringing them back, was much the same as in some of the printed versions; but Mannanan's part at the end was new to me. The old man went on: 'When they came to Ulster, the king made an attack on them, to bring away Deirdre from them; but they killed all that came near them, and drove the whole army back.

'Then the king went to Mannanan of the Hill, and he said: "Come and give me your help against these men, or they will kill the whole army of Ulster." And Mannanan said: "I will give you no help; for I told you all this would come on you if you brought the girl away the time she was a baby in this place." But the king pressed him, and said: "Put blindness on them, the way they will not be able to kill my people."

'So Mannanan agreed to do that, and he put blindness on the three brothers. And when they went out next time to fight against the army, they could not see who was before them; and it was at each other they were striking; and at last all of them fell by each other's hand.

'And when Deirdre saw they were dead, she took up a sword or a dagger that was lying on the ground

and she put it through her own body, and she fell
dead along with them.

'And she was buried on one side of a dry stone
wall, and her husband on the other side. And a briar
grew up on his grave, and a briar on hers ; and they
met over the wall, and joined with one another.'

A young man, narrow-chested and consumptive-
looking, but with fun in his eyes, said then : 'There
were three Irishmen joined the English army, and
they didn't like it. And they were brought to India ;
and when they were there, they agreed to make away.
So they went into a forest, where they would not be
found. And they made a little cabin for themselves
there ; and two of them used to go hunting every
day, and the other would stop at home to make ready
the dinner.

'One day when the pot was on the fire, a little
old man came into the house. " Bum-bum," he said ;
"give me something to eat out of the pot."

'So the soldier gave him a rabbit out of the pot.
" Give me another," he said then. " I will not," said
the soldier ; " for there would not be enough for my
friends' dinner when they come home from hunting."
With that the little man took hold of the pot, and
threw the scalding broth over the .soldier, and made
off, leaving nothing in the pot after him.

' And when the others came home, they found their
comrade lying there on the ground, scalded, and he
told them what had happened.

'The next day the second of them said he would watch the pot. And all happened the same as the first day; and they found him scalded and the pot empty when they came back.

'The third day the third of them said he would keep a watch, and that they might be sure they would get their dinner that evening.

'He put down the pot, and he put the tongs to redden in the fire; and when the pot was boiling, the little man came in. "Bum-bum," he said; "give me a bit from the pot." So the soldier gave him a bit. "Give me more now," he said, when he had the rabbit eaten. "I will not; I will keep it for my comrades," said the soldier. With that the little man took a hold of the pot; but if he did, the soldier took up the tongs that he was after making red-hot in the fire; and the little man made off, and the pot in his arms, and the soldier after him with the tongs. Then the little man dropped the pot; but the soldier took no notice but followed after him till he went down a hole into the ground. Then he took a sapling, and tied his handkerchief on it, and stuck it where the hole was, and went back again to the cabin.

'When his comrades came back, he told them all that happened; and they all set out to where the hole was. And they looked down, and it was very deep; and they could see no end to it. So the third man said to the others: "One of you is a rope-maker, and the other is a cooper; and let you make a rope and a bucket now."

'So they made the rope and the bucket, and fastened one to the other; and the first man was let down.   But after he went a good way, the rope came to an end, and there was no sign of a bottom; and he called to them to pull him up again.   It happened the same with the second man; and he was pulled up again.   Then the third said he would go, and that if the rope would not reach to the bottom, he would take a leap the rest of the way.

'So when the rope was all given out, he made a leap and came safe to the bottom.   And it was in a hole he found himself; and he went through a great many rooms from that, till he came to where the little man was sitting by himself.

'And he gave him a welcome, and said: "You had good courage to get here.   And have you enough courage now," he said, "to go straight before you for three hundred miles, to set free the King of Spain's three daughters that are in the power of three giants?"   "I will do that," said the soldier.

'So the little man gave him directions what to do. "But when you are going to fight the giants," he said, "take no weapon but the little rusty sword you'll find at the back of their own door."

'The soldier set out then; and after he had gone a hundred miles in a straight line, he came to the first castle, and there was a copper crown over it.' (At this, we all looked up at the whitewashed boards of the shed, as if we expected to see the copper crown.) 'And there was a young lady looking out of the window, and she saw him coming. "You'd best not come here," she said: "or the giant that owns the castle will make an end of you." "It's to make an end of himself, I am come," says he, "and to set you free." "And do you think the like of you could stand against him?" says she; "it's what he's gone out for now," says she, "is for seven bullocks to make his dinner of." "I'm ready for him whenever he comes," says the soldier.

'Presently the giant came back, bringing the seven bullocks on his back. "It is to fight me you are come," says he. "Wait till I have my dinner eat, and I'll make a quick end of you."

'So he sat down and had his dinner off the seven bullocks, and then he got up to fight. "What weapons will you fight with?" he says, throwing down a brace of swords. "Is it one of these you will have?" "It is not," said the soldier; "but the little rusty sword that is behind the door."

'So he went in and got that; and the giant began to hit and to strike at him; and he began to tickle the giant's ankles and his calves. And at last the giant stooped down to scratch his ankle; and when he did, the soldier struck off his head.

'He let the princess out then, and bade her to go where the little man was waiting at the bottom of the hole, till he would come to her.'

'He went then to the second castle, that had a silver crown over the door; and then he went on to the third castle, that had a golden crown over the door;

and the same thing happened as before, except that the second giant had fourteen bullocks, and the third giant twenty-one bullocks for his dinner.

'Then he brought the third princess back to the house, at the bottom of the hole, where the little man was sitting. And the little man gave him a whistle, and he blew it; and his comrades came and called down the hole that they were at the top, and he bade them to let the bucket down. And when they did, he put the first of the three princesses in it. They drew her up then; and when they saw so nice a girl come up, they began to quarrel which of them would have her for his wife. "Oh, don't quarrel about me," says she; "for there is a girl much handsomer than myself below yet." So they let the bucket down again, and she made off.

'Then the second princess came up in the bucket, and they began to quarrel for her, and she said : "You may let me go, for I am nothing at all beside the girl that is below in the hole yet."

'So they let her go; and then the third princess that was the most beautiful came up, and they began to quarrel for her. "You need not be quarrelling for me," says she ; "for it is your comrade that is at the bottom of the hole yet, I am going to marry."

'So when they heard that, they let the bucket down again. But when the soldier below was going to get into it, the little man said : " Don't get in," he said ; " but put stones in it ; for your comrades will cut the rope when it is half way up."

'So he filled it with stones, and sure enough, when it was half way up, his comrades cut the rope, and the bucket fell to the bottom.'

('Oh! oh! oh!' There were indignant murmurs among the old men at this.)

'The soldier did not know then what way he would make his escape. But the little old man took his whistle, and blew on it ; and presently a great big eagle came down the hole.

'The little man bade the soldier get on its back till it would bring him across the world ; and he put seven bullocks on its back along with him.

'They set out then ; and the soldier was cutting a bit off the bullocks and putting it into the eagle's beak whenever he would say "Quawk." But they were only a third of the way when all was gone, and they had to turn back again.

'He took fourteen bullocks the next time, but they gave out. But the third time the little old man gave twenty-one bullocks.

'So this time the eagle brought him to Spain, and left him down there. And at that time the King of Spain was making a great feast for the marriage of his eldest daughter that was the most beautiful. And when the soldier saw her, he knew she was the third of the princesses he had set free from the giant, and the other two were her two sisters.

'It was given out then that the princess would not marry anyone but the man that would bring her a golden crown, the same as the one that was hung

N

over the castle where the giant had kept her. And
all the goldsmiths were very busy, everyone employ-
ing them to make crowns. But they could not make
the right one.

'Now the little man had given the soldier a ring
before they parted, and had bade him rub it if he
would want anything from him. So he rubbed it,
and a genii appeared before him. "Master, master,
best master, what is your will?" "Bring me the
golden crown from the third castle where I killed the
giant," says the soldier.

'So the genii brought it; and Jack went to the
king's court and put it down; and the princess said it
was just the very same crown that was over the
castle; and she knew it was the soldier had freed
her, and she was willing to marry him.

'But the king was not pleased to see such a poor-
looking husband coming for his daughter; and he
said he would give her to no one but a man that
would bring a coach for her.

'So the soldier went away, and he rubbed the ring,
and the genii appeared; and it is what he bade him,
to get him a coach that would be filled full up of
mud. So the coach went up to the king's door, and
the king himself came out to open it; and when he
did, out came all the mud over him that he was near
choked. And he filled it a second and a third time
with pebbles and with stones, and the same thing
happened.

'Then the soldier bade the genii to bring him a

fine empty coach, and he got into it. And when he was in it, it is what he wished, to have the princess sitting beside him.

'And there she was on the minute, and they went away together. But the king gave his consent then, and a great deal of money and treasure.

'And they put down the teapot, and if they didn't live happy'—the end was lost in applause.

And when the applause had died away, an old, bright-eyed wrinkled man, said : 'There was a King of Leinster one time, and there was a lake beside his house. And every now and again twelve swans used to come to the lake ; and they had been coming there for seven generations.

'And the king's son that was away came home. And one day he saw the swans coming to the lake ; and he said : "I wonder I never heard any talk of these swans before, for they are the most beautiful I ever saw." And his people said : "They are coming here for seven generations, and no one ever took notice of them before."

'The next morning early the king's son went down and hid himself in the flags and the rushes by the lake. And after he had watched for a while, he saw the swans come flying to the edge of the lake. And then they took off their flying habits, and went bathing in the water ; and they were not swans but beautiful young women ; and there was one among them that was the most beautiful of all.

' After the king's son had watched for a while, he
went to where they had left their flying habits ; and he
orought away the one that belonged to the most
beautiful of the women.   After a while they came to
shore, and began to look for their flying habits,
and when she could not find hers, she made great
laments.

' The king's son came out to her then ; and he asked
her would she stop with him and be his wife.   " I
cannot do that," she said ; " but give me back my
wings now, and if you will come to the shore at such
a place to-morrow, I will bring a ship, and you can
come away with me.   So he gave her back her habit,
and she took the form of a swan again and flew
away.

' The next day he was making ready for his journey
before he would go to meet her ; and the old woman
that was in the house, and that was over eighty years
old, came and asked could she go with him.   So at
last he gave her leave, and they went down to the
shore to wait.   And the nurse said : " Lie down
now and put your head in my lap and rest awhile."
So he laid his head in her lap ; and when he did that,
she took a sleeping-pin and put it in his ear, and he
fell into a heavy sleep.

' And when he was asleep, the ship came over the
sea, with music and playing in it, and came near the
land.   And when there was no one to meet it there,
it went away again.

' The king's son awoke then, and the nurse said :

" It is making a fool of you she was, for we have waited here all the day, and there has no ship come."

'So they went back home; but the next day he went down to the shore again, and the same thing happened. The young man lay down to rest, and the nurse put a sleeping-pin in his ear, and the ship came when he was asleep, and it went away again.

'But this time the lady in the ship wrote a letter and left it on the strand; and when the king's son awoke, and that the nurse told him there had no ship come, he was distracted, and went wandering about on the strand, and there he found the letter; and it told him what to do, and the way the nurse had deceived him.

'So the next day when he went to the shore and the nurse followed him, he brought her where there was a well, and put a stone about her neck and pushed her in, and she was seen no more.

'Then he went down to the shore, and he met the lady; but she said : " I cannot bring you with me now, but I will leave the ship with you, and you must follow till you find me."

'And he took the ship, and she gave him directions; and he went on till he came to a country a long way off, and a wood in it, and a house in the wood, and an old man sitting in it.

'And he told the old man all that had happened, and how he was looking for the lady. And the old man gave him clothes to put on, and a place to wash

himself, till he was as fresh and fair as before he set
out.

'And then he sent for a pony, and he said : " I
will give you this pony that will bring you where she
is ; and when you get there, you must put the bridle
on his neck, and put the saddle cross-ways, and turn
his head back here again.

'So then he got on the pony's back ; and it flew
away with him through the air, till at last it put him
down on land, near a great castle. And he turned
the saddle cross-ways, and put the bridle on the
pony's neck, and turned its head, and it went back
to where it came from.

'Then he went on to the castle ; and he went in and
asked the Master to take him as a serving-man.
And the Master said he would, and he said : " The
work you have to do to-night is to attend to the
horse that is in the stable, and that belongs to my
daughter."

'But before the young man did that, he went to
look for the young lady, and he saw her looking out
of a window ; and he went up to her, and she knew
him, and gave him a welcome. And she said : " The
Master of the house knows well who you are, and
that it is to bring me away you are come ; and that
is the reason he bade you go to clean and to attend
to the horse in the stable ; for it is wicked, and it
would make an end of you. But," says she, " take
these brushes and these shammys and bring them
along with you into the stable, and the horse will be

as quiet as a lamb ; and in place of wanting to kill
you, he will love you. And when night comes," says
she, " he will come to us, and we will get on his back,
and he will bring us away."

'So all happened as she said, and the horse came
at night, and they both of them got on his back ;
and away with him, and never stopped till he brought
them back to Ireland, and to this country.

'And it was in this country they settled down ;
and some of their descendants are living in it yet.'

'What is their name ?'

'Well, I think they are the Persses of Roxborough ;
or maybe they are the Gregorys of Coole.'

A red-faced, farmer-like man says : 'There was a
poor man one time—Jack Murphy his name was ; and
rent day came, and he hadn't enough to pay his rent.
And he went to the landlord, and asked would he
give him time. And the landlord asked when would
he pay him ; and he said he didn't know that. And
the landlord said : "Well, if you can answer three
questions I'll put to you, I'll let you off the rent
altogether. But if you don't answer them, you will
have to pay it at once, or to leave your farm. And
the three questions are these :—How much does the
moon weigh ? How many stars are there in the
sky ? What is it I am thinking?" And he said he
would give him till the next day to think of the
answers.

'And Jack was walking along, very downhearted ;

and he met with a friend of his, one Tim Daly; and he asked what was on him; and he told him how he must answer the landlord's three questions on to-morrow, or to lose his farm. " And I see no use in going to him to-morrow," says he; " for I 'm sure I will not be able to answer his questions right." " Let me go in your place," says Tim Daly; " for the landlord will not know one of us from the other; and I 'm a good hand at answering questions, and I 'll engage I 'll get you through."

'So he agreed to that; and the next day Tim Daly went in to the landlord, and says he: " I 'm come now to answer your three questions."

'Well, the first question the landlord put was: " What does the moon weigh?" And Tim Daly says: " It weighs four quarters."

' Then the landlord asked: " How many stars are in the sky?" " Nine thousand nine hundred and ninety-nine," says Tim. " How do you know that?" says the landlord. " Well," says Tim, " if you don't believe me, go out yourself to-night and count them."

' Then the landlord asked him the third question: " What am I thinking now?" " You are thinking it 's to Jack Murphy you're talking, and it is not, but to Tim Daly."

' So the landlord gave in then; and Jack had the farm free from that out.'

There was great laughter and applause at this story.

Then someone told this version of the *Taming of the Shrew*. I heard it told in Irish afterwards by an Aran girl at the Galway Feis:

' There was a farmer one time had three daughters ; and two of them were very nice and civil, but the third had a very hot temper. And the two civil ones were married first ; and then a gentleman came and asked for the third. So after the wedding they started for home ; and the farmer said to his son-in-law : " God speed you—yourself and your Fireball."

' Well, on the way home, a hare started up ; and the gentleman had a white hound, and it followed the hare ; and he called to it to leave following it, but it would not till it had it killed. And it came back then, and the gentleman took out his pistol and shot the hound dead. " I did that because it would not obey me," he said.

' And after a little time they came to a stone wall that was very high ; and he put the white horse he was riding at it, and the horse refused it, and he shot it dead. " I did that because he would not take the wall when I bade him," he said.

' They came home then ; and there was a good deal of feasting made, and of good treatment for all the servants in the house ; but as to the wife she got hardly enough given her, and that of the worst. She was angry then ; and she said to the husband : " Why am I badly treated this way, and your servants are well treated ?" " I have a good reason for that," says he ; " for my servants are working hard for me, and

doing all they can for me, and you are doing nothing
at all."

'Well, whatever happened after that, all the daughters and the sons-in-law came back one time to the
father's house to see him.   And after the dinner, the
daughters were playing cards together, and the sons-
in-law were in another room with the father.   And
he asked the first of them how did he like his wife.
" Very well," says he, " I have no fault to find with
her, a very civil, obedient girl."   The second son-in-
law said the same; and then the father said to the man
that married the hot-tempered one : " And what sort
of an account have you to give of your missus ?"
" Very good," he said.   " If her sisters are civil and
obedient, she is three times more civil and obedient."

' They were surprised to hear him say that ; and
they said they would put it to the proof.   And the
first husband went to the door and called to his wife,
"Come here a minute."   "I can't come," says she; "I'm
dealing the cards."   Then the second husband went
and called to his wife that he wanted her.   " I can't
come," says she ; " I'm playing the game."   Then the
third went and called to his wife ; and she rose up and
put down the cards, and came out to him on the
moment.   "What were you doing when I called you ?"
says he.   " I was playing the game," says she.

' They all wondered when they heard that, and
they asked what made her, that was so hard to
manage before, so quiet now.

'" I will tell you that," she said.   And she told

them the whole story of the horse and the hound being shot, and the servants being treated better than herself.

'And that's the end of my story.'

Then a young red-faced, one-eyed man was dragged forward, and he said:

'There was a farmer one time had met with great misfortunes; and at last of all his stock he had nothing left but one cow. And when he saw his children starving with the hunger, he made up his mind to sell the cow, and he set out with her to the fair.

'And on the road he met a man that asked would he sell the cow. "I will indeed; it's for that I'm going to the fair," says he. "Will you give her to me for this bottle?" says the man, holding out a bottle to him. "Do you know what my wife would do if I brought her home that bottle in place of the cow?" said the farmer. "I do not," said the man. "She'd break it on my head," said the farmer.

'Well, the man pressed him for a while; and at last he said the fair might be a bad one, and maybe he might as well chance the bottle and go home. So he took the bottle and gave the cow in place of it, and went home.

'When his wife knew what he had done, she went near losing her wits; and she called him all the names; and the children were crying with the hunger. And the poor man didn't know what to do; and he sat down, and he put the bottle on the table and opened it.

'And as soon as he did that, two men came out of it, and they began to lay a cloth, and to set out every sort of food on it. And the man and his wife and the children sat down and eat their fill.

'And everything the farmer would wish for after that, he had but to open the bottle and the two men would come out, and would bring him what he wanted. So he grew to be rich, and the neighbours heard how he came by his money. And his landlord got word of it, and he came and asked would he sell the bottle to him.

' But he refused to part with it ; but after a while the landlord got him to his own house, and gave him drink; and, not being in his clear senses, he consented to give up the bottle for four acres of good land.

' But after a while he had all his riches spent, and someway nothing went well with him ; and at last he found himself the same way he was before, with but one cow left of all his stock, and the children crying with hunger.

' So he set off with the one cow; and he went to the same place he met with the man with the bottle before, and he was there before him. And he told him all that had happened, and the way it was with him now ; and the man gave him another bottle, and brought away the cow.

' So he hurried back home with the bottle, and set it on the table and drew the cork, and the children were waiting round the table for the good dinner they would have. But when the bottle was opened, two men came out with blackthorns in their hands, and they began to beat the farmer and his wife and all about them ; and it was blows the poor children got in place of food.

'Well, as soon as the men went into the bottle again, the farmer put in the cork, and he went away to the landlord's house. And there was a great ball going on there; and the farmer asked could he see the landlord.

' So he came down to him, and the farmer said he had got a new bottle, and that maybe the ladies and gentlemen would like to see all it would do. So the landlord agreed, and brought him up to the ballroom, and he put down the bottle and opened the cork. And when it was open, the two men came out with their blackthorns, and they began to hit at the ladies and gentlemen near them, and to beat them, till they ran to hide in every corner. And the landlord called out for them to stop, but the farmer said they would not till he would get his own bottle again.

' So they gave it to him then, and he went home bringing the two bottles with him. And he lived in plenty ever after till he died.

' But someway at his wake, with all that was going on there, the two bottles got broken, or if they did not they were lost.'

Then another said : ' There was a servant-girl left to mind her master's house one time. And she heard a noise below the window, and she opened it to look out. And she saw the hand of a man on the window ledge, that was climbing up to rob the house. And when he put his hand up, she took a little hatchet she had and cut his hand off.

'The same thing happened with another man, and another after him again, till she had killed six. But when she was striking at the seventh, he drew back, and all she cut off was his finger.

'When the master came back, she got great praise and great reward, so that she had plenty of money. And one day a man came to ask her in marriage ; and she did not know him to be the robber that escaped, and she married him.

'But after a while he brought her out through the fields to where there was a little bridge over the river. And when they got to it, he told her he was the man she had cut the finger off, and that he had brought her there to kill her.

'"Give me time to say my prayers first," she said. So he gave her time for that, and she knelt down ; and presently she turned round and he was on the bridge beside her, and she gave him a push into the water. And that was the end of the seventh of the robbers.

'And then she went home again. That's my story.'

And then the old man, whose brother has fought for the king, and hasn't sent him anything, said :

'Peace is made. That's my story. Will you give me tobacco for that?'

But this being the last day, they all had tobacco—story-tellers and all.

And here is the last story : ' There was a steward one time in the employment of a gentleman ; and he was a good, honourable man. And he used to make the Sunday begin at twelve o'clock on Saturday ; and to ring the bell then for the workmen to go home.

' He got sick at last, and his death was drawing near ; and he asked one request of his master, and that was, that after his death he would put his body on a car, but not direct it anywhere ; but to let it go what way the horse would bring it.

' So the master did that ; and they put the body on a car, and the carman went along with it ; but he did not direct the horse, but let it go what way it liked.

' And it went on a long way; and then they came to a path that was all full of spearheads sticking up through the ground. But the horse went on ; and wherever it went, the spearheads would sink away before it.

' They came at last to a house, and the horse stopped at the door ; and the people of the house came out and brought in the body ; and the carman went along with it, and he lay down and slept awhile.

' And when he rose up, he said he would go back to his friends. But the people of the house said : " You can go back if you like, but you will find none of your friends before you ; for your sleep has lasted for seven hundred years."

'So he went back ; and there was nothing but grass and bushes in the village he came from. And he knelt down and made his repentance ; and he was let up to heaven for the sake of the steward that was so good, and that made the Sunday begin at noon on Saturday.'

1902.

ON THE EDGE OF THE WORLD

JUST where the road that runs by the bay turns northward to run by the Atlantic, a few white houses on either side turn it for a moment into a street. The grey road was not all grey yesterday, in spite of stones, and sea, and clouds, and a mist that blotted out the hills ; for July had edged it with yellow rag-weed, the horses of the Sidhe, and with purple heather ; and besides the tireless turf-laden donkeys, there were men in white and women in crimson flannel going towards the village. One woman sitting in a donkey-cart was chanting a song in Irish about a voyage across the sea ; and when someone asked her if she was to try for a prize at the *Feis*, the Irish festival going on in the village, she only answered that she was 'lonesome after the old times.'

At the *Feis*, in the white schoolhouse, some boys and girls from schools and convents at the ' big town ' many miles away were singing ; and now and then a little bare-footed boy from close by would go up on the platform and sing the *Paistin Fionn*, or *Is truag gan Peata*. People from the scattered houses

O

and villages about had gathered to listen ; some had
come in turf-boats from Aran, Irish speakers, proud
to show that the language that has been called dead
has never died ; and glad at the new life that is
coming into it. Men in loose flannel-jackets sang
old songs, many sad ones, but not all ; for one that
was addressed to a mother, who had broken off her
daughter's marriage with the maker of the song,
turned more to anger than to grief ; and there was
the love song, 'Courteous Bridget,' made perhaps a
hundred years ago, by wandering Raftery.

A woman with madder-dyed petticoat sang the
lament of an emigrant going across the great sea,
telling how she got up at daybreak to look at
the places she was going to leave, Ballinrobe and
the rest ; and how she envied the birds that were
free of the air, and the beasts that were free of the
mountain, and were not forced to go away. Another
song that was sung was the Jacobite one, with the
refrain that has been put into English—'Seagan
O'Dwyer a Gleanna, we're worsted in the game!'

Some poems were repeated also : Raftery's 'Argument with whiskey,' in which he puts the joys and
sorrows of its lovers only too impartially. Another
'Argument' was between two men, herds, I think ;
each counting up the virtues of his own province,
Connaught or Munster. An old man gave a long
poem, a recital of Bible history ; but the judges rang
their bell when he had got to the parable of the
Prodigal Son, and was telling how 'the poor foolish

boy went away from his home and from his father to some far country'; and he left the platform saying indignantly: 'You might have left me time to bring him back again.' And there was a poem on 'The rising again of Ireland,' telling how, when she has risen, 'ships will be coming to her from France and from Spain, and from all the countries; and there will be no rent on the land; and every poet will be given a fee of twenty-one pounds.'

In the evening there were people waiting round the door to hear the songs and the pipes again. An old man among them was speaking with many gestures, his voice rising, and a crowd gathering about him. '*Tha se beo, tha se beo*'—'he is living, he is living,' I heard him say over and over again. I asked what he was saying, and was told: 'He says that Parnell is alive yet.' I was pushed away from him by the crowd to where a policeman was looking on. 'He says that Parnell is alive still,' I said. 'There are many say that,' he answered. 'And, after all, no one ever saw the body that was buried.'

The rising again of Ireland, of her old speech, of her last leader, dreams all, as we are told. But here, on the edge of the world, dreams are real things, and every heart is watching for the opening of one or another grave.

AN CRAOIBHIN'S PLAYS

I HOLD that the beginning of modern Irish drama
was in the winter of 1898, at a school feast at Coole,
when Douglas Hyde and Miss Norma Borthwick
acted in Irish in a Punch and Judy show; and the
delighted children went back to tell their parents
what grand curses *An Craoibhin* had put on the baby
and the policeman.

A little time after that, when a play was wanted
for our Literary Theatre, Dr. Hyde wrote, and then
acted in, 'The Twisting of the Rope,' the first Irish
play ever given in a Dublin theatre.

It has been acted many times since then, in Dublin,
in London, in Galway, in Galway Workhouse, in
Cornamona, Ballaghaderreen, Ballymoe, and other
places. It has always given great delight, and its
success is very natural; for the Irish-speakers, who
are its audience, have an inborn love of drama, as is
shown by their handing down of such long dramatic
dialogues as those between Oisin and St. Patrick,
from century to century. At country gatherings,
those old dialogues, and the newer ones between
Death and Raftery, or between the farmers of two

provinces, are followed with a patient joy ; and the creation of acting plays is the natural outcome of this living tradition. And Douglas Hyde's dramas grow directly from the folk-memory. The tradition and the beautiful old air, and the song of ' The Twisting of the Rope,' are very well known :—

' What was the dead cat that put me in this place,
  And all the pretty young girls I left after me ?
  I came into the house where was the bright love of my heart ;
  And the old hag put me out by the Twisting of the Rope.

' If you are mine, be mine by day and by night ;
  If you are mine, be mine before the world ;
  If you are mine, be mine with every inch of your heart ;
  It is my grief you are not with me as a wife this evening.

' It is down in Sligo I got knowledge of my love ;
  It is up in Galway I drank my fill with her.
  By the strength of my hands, if they do not leave me as I
    am,
  I will do a trick will set these women walking.'

Mr. Yeats made Red Hanrahan the hero of this song in a story in ' The Secret Rose ' ; and it is Hanrahan Douglas Hyde has kept in the play, with his passion, his exaggerations, his wheedling tongue, his roving heart, that all but coax the girl from her mother and her sweetheart ; but that fail after all in their attack on the settled order of things, and leave their owner homeless and restless, and angry and chiding, like the stormy west wind outside the door.

'The Marriage' is founded on the story of Raftery at the poor wedding at Cappaghtagle. It was acted in Galway, at the *Feis*, last summer. There had been some delay or misunderstanding in the giving of parts ; and on the morning of the *Feis*, it was announced that the play would not be given. But the disappointment was so great, that we all begged *An Craoibhin* to take the chief part himself, as he had done in 'The Twisting of the Rope'; and when his kindness made him agree to this, we went in search of the other players. They were all at work in shops or stores, one wheeling sacks on a barrow ; and it was a busy market-day, and it was hard for them to get away for a rehearsal. But, for all that, the play was given in the evening ; in the very town where some still remember Raftery, and where he and Death had their first talk together.

It will be hard to forget the blind poet, as he was represented on the stage by the living poet, so full of kindly humour, of humorous malice, of dignity under his poor clothing, or the wistful, ghostly sigh with which he went out of the door at the end. 'ⁱſ ſeaſ maſᵬ ᴅo ᵬí ann '—'It is a dead man was in it.'

It has been acted in Dublin since then ; and many places are asking for the loan of the one manuscript in which it exists ; but I am glad Connacht had it first.

'The Lost Saint' was written last summer. *An Craoibhin* was staying with us at Coole ; and one morning I went for a long drive to the sea, leaving

him with a bundle of blank paper before him. When
I came back at evening, I was told that Dr. Hyde
had finished his play, and was out shooting wild
duck. The hymn, however, was not quite ready, and
was put into rhyme next day, while he was again
watching for wild duck beside Inchy marsh.

When he read it to us in the evening, we were all
left with a feeling as if some beautiful white blossom
had suddenly fallen at our feet.

It was acted the other day at Ballaghaderreen ;
and, at the end, a very little girl, who wanted to let
the author know how much she had liked his play,
put out her hand, and put a piece of toffee into his.

The ' Nativity ' did not appear in time for Christmas acting ; but Ireland, which now and then finds
herself possessed of some accidental freedom, has no
censor ; and a play so beautiful and reverent, and so
much in the tradition of the people, is sure to be
acted and received reverently.

An Craoibhin has written other plays besides these
—a pastoral play which has been acted in Dublin
and Belfast, a match-making comedy, a satire on
Trinity College.

Other Irish plays have been acted here and there
through the country during the last year or two,
some written by priests ; the last I saw in manuscript was by a workhouse schoolmaster; and all have
had their share of success. But it is to the poet-
scholar who has become actor-dramatist that we
must still, as Raftery would put it, ' give the branch.'

THE TWISTING OF THE ROPE

HANRAHAN. *A wandering poet.*
SHEAMUS O'HERAN. *Engaged to* OONA.
MAURYA. *The woman of the house.*
SHEELA. *A neighbour.*
OONA. *Maurya's daughter.*
Neighbours and a piper who have come to Maurya's house for a dance.

SCENE. *A farmer's house in Munster a hundred years ago. Men and women moving about and standing round the walls as if they had just finished a dance.* HANRAHAN, *in the foreground, talking to* OONA.

The piper is beginning a preparatory drone for another dance, but SHEAMUS *brings him a drink and he stops. A man has come and holds out his hand to* OONA, *as if to lead her out, but she pushes him away.*

OONA. Don't be bothering me now; don't you see I'm listening to what he is saying? (*To* HANRAHAN) Go on with what you were saying just now.

HANRAHAN. What did that fellow want of you?

OONA. He wanted the next dance with me, but I wouldn't give it to him.

HANRAHAN. And why would you give it to him? Do you think I'd let you dance with anyone but myself, and I here? I had no comfort or satisfaction this long time until I came here to-night, and till I saw yourself.

OONA. What comfort am I to you?

HANRAHAN. When a stick is half burned in the fire, does it not get comfort when water is poured on it?

OONA. But, sure, you are not half burned.

HANRAHAN. I am; and three-quarters of my heart is burned, and scorched and consumed, struggling with the world, and the world struggling with me.

OONA. You don't look that bad.

HANRAHAN. O, Oona ni Regaun, you have not knowledge of the life of a poor bard, without house or home or havings, but he going and ever going a drifting through the wide world, without a person with him but himself. There is not a morning in the week when I rise up that I do not say to myself that it would be better to be in the grave than to be wandering. There is nothing standing to me but the gift I got from God, my share of songs; when I begin upon them, my grief and my trouble go from me; I forget my persecution and my ill luck; and now since I saw you, Oona, I see there is something that is better even than the songs.

OONA. Poetry is a wonderful gift from God; and

as long as you have that, you are richer than the people of stock and store, the people of cows and cattle.

HANRAHAN. Ah, Oona, it is a great blessing, but it is a great curse as well for a man, he to be a poet. Look at me : have I a friend in this world ?   Is there a man alive that has a wish for me ? is there the love of anyone at all on me ?   I am going like a poor lonely barnacle goose throughout the world ; like Oisin after the Fenians ; every person hates me : you do not hate me, Oona ?

OONA. Do not say a thing like that ; it is impossible that anyone would hate you.

HANRAHAN. Come and we will sit in the corner of the room together ; and I will tell you the little song I made for you ; it is for you I made it.   (*They go to a corner and sit down together.*   SHEELA *comes in at the door.*)

SHEELA. I came to you as quick as I could.

MAURYA. And a hundred welcomes to you.

SHEELA. What have you going on now?

MAURYA. Beginning we are ; we had one jig, and now the piper is drinking a glass.   They'll begin dancing again in a minute when the piper is ready.

SHEELA. There are a good many people gathering in to you to-night.   We will have a fine dance.

MAURYA. Maybe so, Sheela ; but there's a man of them there, and I'd sooner him out than in.

SHEELA. It's about the long red man you are talking, isn't it—the man that is in close talk with

Oona in the corner? Where is he from, and who is he himself?

MAURYA. That's the greatest vagabond ever came into Ireland; Tumaus Hanrahan they call him; but it's Hanrahan the rogue he ought to have been christened by right. Aurah, wasn't there the misfortune on me, him to come in to us at all to-night?

SHEELA. What sort of a person is he? Isn't he a man that makes songs, out of Connacht? I heard talk of him before; and they say there is not another dancer in Ireland so good as him. I would like to see him dance.

MAURYA. Bad luck to the vagabond! It is well I know what sort he is; because there was a kind of friendship between himself and the first husband I had; and it is often I heard from poor Diarmuid—the Lord have mercy on him!—what sort of person he was. He was a schoolmaster down in Connacht; but he used to have every trick worse than another; ever making songs he used to be, and drinking whiskey and setting quarrels afoot among the neighbours with his share of talk. They say there isn't a woman in the five provinces that he wouldn't deceive. He is worse than Donal na Greina long ago. But the end of the story is that the priest routed him out of the parish altogether; he got another place then, and followed on at the same tricks until he was routed out again, and another again with it. Now he has neither place nor house nor anything, but he to be going the country, making songs and getting a night's lodging from the people; nobody will refuse him, because they are afraid of him. He's a great poet, and maybe he'd make a rann on you that would stick to you for ever, if you were to anger him.

SHEELA. God preserve us; but what brought him in to-night?

MAURYA. He was travelling the country and he heard there was to be a dance here, and he came in because he knew us; he was rather great with my first husband. It is wonderful how he is making out his way of life at all, and he with nothing but his share of songs. They say there is no place that he'll go to, that the women don't love him, and that the men don't hate him.

SHEELA (*catching* MAURYA *by the shoulder*). Turn your head, Maurya; look at him now, himself and your daughter, and their heads together; he's whispering in her ear; he's after making a poem for her and he's whispering it in her ear. Oh, the villain, he'll be putting his spells on her now.

MAURYA. Ohone, go deo! isn't it a misfortune that he came? He's talking every moment with Oona since he came in three hours ago. I did my best to separate them from one another, but it failed me. Poor Oona is given up to every sort of old songs and old made-up stories; and she thinks it sweet to be listening to him. The marriage is settled between herself and Sheamus O'Herin there, a quarter from to-day. Look at poor Sheamus at the door, and he watching them. There is grief and hanging of the head on him; it's easy to see that he'd like to choke the vagabond this minute. I am greatly afraid that the head will be turned on Oona with his share of blathering. As sure as I am alive there will come evil out of this night.

SHEELA. And couldn't you put him out?

MAURYA. I could. There's no person here to help him unless there would be a woman or two; but he is a great poet, and he has a curse that would split the trees, and that would burst the stones. They say the seed will rot in the ground and the milk go from the cows when a poet like him makes a curse, if a person routed him out of the house; but if he was once out, I'll go bail I wouldn't let him in again.

SHEELA. If himself were to go out willingly, there would be no virtue in his curse then.

MAURYA. There would not, but he will not go out willingly, and I cannot rout him out myself for fear of his curse.

SHEELA. Look at poor Sheamus. He is going over to her. (SHEAMUS *gets up and goes over to her.*)

SHEAMUS. Will you dance this reel with me, Oona, as soon as the piper is ready?

HANRAHAN (*rising up*). I am Tumaus Hanrahan, and I am speaking now to Oona ni Regaun; and as she is willing to be talking to me, I will allow no living person to come between us.

SHEAMUS (*without heeding* HANRAHAN). Will you not dance with me, Oona?

HANRAHAN (*savagely*). Didn't I tell you now that

it was to me Oona ni Regaun was talking? Leave
that on the spot, you clown, and do not raise a
disturbance here.

SHEAMUS. Oona——

HANRAHAN (*shouting*). Leave that! (SHEAMUS
goes away, and comes over to the two old women.)

SHEAMUS. Maurya Regaun, I am asking leave
of you to throw that ill-mannerly, drunken vagabond
out of the house. Myself and my two brothers will
put him out if you will allow us; and when he's
outside I'll settle with him.

MAURYA. Sheamus, do not; I am afraid of him.
That man has a curse they say that would split the trees.

SHEAMUS. I don't care if he had a curse that would
overthrow the heavens; it is on me it will fall, and I
defy him! If he were to kill me on the moment, I
will not allow him to put his spells on Oona. Give
me leave, Mauyra.

SHEELA. Do not, Sheamus. I have a better advice
than that.

SHEAMUS. What advice is that?

SHEELA. I have a way in my head to put him out.
If you follow my advice, he will go out himself as
quiet as a lamb; and when you get him out, slap the
door on him, and never let him in again.

MAUYRA. Luck from God on you, Sheela, and tell
us what's in your head.

SHEELA. We will do it as nice and easy as you
ever saw. We will put him to twist a hay-rope till
he is outside, and then we will shut the door on him.

SHEAMUS. It's easy to say, but not easy to do. He will say to you, " Make a hay-rope yourself."

SHEELA. We will say then that no one ever saw a hay-rope made, that there is no one at all in the house to make the beginning of it.

SHEAMUS. But will *he* believe that we never saw a hay-rope ?

SHEELA. He believe it, is it ? He'd believe anything ; he'd believe that himself is king over Ireland when he has a glass taken, as he has now.

SHEAMUS. But what excuse can we make for saying we want a hay-rope ?

MAURYA. Can't you think of something yourself, Sheamus ?

SHEAMUS. Sure, I can say the wind is rising, and I must bind the thatch, or it will be off the house.

SHEELA. But he'll know the wind is not rising if he does but listen at the door. You must think of some other excuse, Sheamus.

SHEAMUS. Wait, I have a good idea now ; say there is a coach upset at the bottom of the hill, and that they are asking for a hay-rope to mend it with. He can't see as far as that from the door, and he won't know it's not true it is.

MAURYA. That's the story, Sheela. Now, Sheamus, go among the people and tell them the secret. Tell them what they have to say, that no one at all in this country ever saw a hay-rope, and put a good skin on the lie yourself. (SHEAMUS *goes from person to person whispering to them, and some of them begin laughing.*

The piper has begun playing. Three or four couples rise up.)

HANRAHAN (*after looking at them for a couple of minutes*). Whisht! Let ye sit down! Do ye call that dragging, dancing? You are tramping the floor like so many cattle. You are as heavy as bullocks, as awkward as asses. May my throat be choked if I would not sooner be looking at as many lame ducks hopping on one leg through the house. Leave the floor to Oona ni Regaun and to me.

ONE OF THE MEN GOING TO DANCE. And for what would we leave the floor to you?

HANRAHAN. The swan of the brink of the waves, the royal phœnix, the pearl of the white breast, the Venus amongst the women, Oona ni Regaun, is standing up with me, and any place she rises up, the sun and the moon bow to her, and so shall ye yet. She is too handsome, too sky-like for any other woman to be near her. But wait a while! Before I'll show you how the Connacht boy can dance, I will give you the poem I made on the star of the province of Munster, on Oona ni Regaun. Get up, O sun among women, and we will sing the song together, verse about, and then we'll show them what right dancing is! (OONA *rises.*)

HANRAHAN.

She is white Oona of the yellow hair,
The Coolin that was destroying my heart inside me ;
She is my secret love and my lasting affection ;
I care not for ever for any woman but her.

OONA.

O bard of the black eye, it is you
Who have found victory in the world and fame ;
I call on yourself and I praise your mouth ;
You have set my heart in my breast astray.

HANRAHAN.

O fair Oona of the golden hair,
My desire, my affection, my love and my store,
Herself will go with her bard afar ;
She has hurt his heart in his breast greatly.

OONA.

I would not think the night long nor the day,
Listening to your fine discourse ;
More melodious is your mouth than the singing of
   the birds ;
From my heart in my breast you have found love.

HANRAHAN.

I walked myself the entire world,
England, Ireland, France, and Spain ;
I never saw at home or afar
Any girl under the sun like fair Oona.

OONA.

I have heard the melodious harp
On the streets of Cork playing to us ;
More melodious by far I thought your voice,
More melodious by far your mouth than that.

P

HANRAHAN.

I was myself one time a poor barnacle goose ;
The night was not plain to me more than the day
Till I got sight of her ; she is the love of my heart
That banished from me my grief and my misery.

OONA.

I was myself on the morning of yesterday
Walking beside the wood at the break of day ;
There was a bird there was singing sweetly,
How I love love, and is it not beautiful ?

(*A shout and a noise, and* SHEAMUS O'HERAN
rushes in.)

SHEAMUS. Ububu! Ohone-y-o, go deo! The big
coach is overthrown at the foot of the hill ! The bag
in which the letters of the country are is bursted; and
there is neither tie, nor cord, nor rope, nor anything
to bind it up. They are calling out now for a hay
sugaun—whatever kind of thing that is ; the letters
and the coach will be lost for want of a hay sugaun
to bind them.

HANRAHAN. Do not be bothering us ; we have
our poem done, and we are going to dance. The
coach does not come this way at all.

SHEAMUS. The coach does come this way now ;
but sure you're a stranger, and you don't know.
Doesn't the coach come over the hill now, neighbours?

ALL. It does, it does, surely.

HANRAHAN. I don't care whether it does come

or whether it doesn't.   I would sooner twenty coaches
to be overthrown on the road than the pearl of the
white breast to be stopped from dancing to us.   Tell
the coachman to twist a rope for himself.

SHEAMUS. Oh! murder! he can't.   There's that
much vigour, and fire, and activity, and courage in the
horses, that my poor coachman must take them by
the heads; it's on the pinch of his life he's able to
control them; he's afraid of his soul they'll go from
him of a rout.   They are neighing like anything; you
never saw the like of them for wild horses.

HANRAHAN. Are there no other people in the
coach that will make a rope, if the coachman has to
be at the horses' heads?   Leave that, and let us
dance.

SHEAMUS. There are three others in it; but as to
one of them, he is one-handed, and another man of
them, he's shaking and trembling with the fright he
got; it's not in him now to stand up on his two
feet with the fear that's on him; and as for the third
man, there isn't a person in this country would speak
to him about a rope at all, for his own father was
hanged with a rope last year for stealing sheep.

HANRAHAN. Then let one of yourselves twist a
rope so, and leave the floor to us.   (*To* OONA.) Now,
O star of women, show me how Juno goes among
the gods, or Helen for whom Troy was destroyed.
By my word, since Deirdre died, for whom Naoise,
son of Usnech, was put to death, her heir is not in
Ireland to-day but yourself.   Let us begin.

SHEAMUS. Do not begin until we have a rope; we are not able to twist a rope; there's nobody here can twist a rope.

HANRAHAN. There's nobody here is able to twist a rope?

ALL. Nobody at all.

SHEELA. And that's true; nobody in this place ever made a hay sugaun. I don't believe there's a person in this house who ever saw one itself but me. It's well I remember when I was a little girsha that I saw one of them on a goat that my grandfather brought with him out of Connacht. All the people used to be saying: " Aurah, what sort of a thing is that at all?" And he said that it was a sugaun that was in it; and that people used to make the like of that down in Connacht. He said that one man would go holding the hay, and another man twisting it. I'll hold the hay now; and you'll go twisting it.

SHEAMUS. I'll bring in a lock of hay. (*He goes out.*)

HANRAHAN.

I will make a dispraising of the province of Munster:
They do not leave the floor to us;
It isn't in them to twist even a sugaun;
The province of Munster without nicety, without prosperity.

Disgust for ever on the province of Munster,
That they do not leave us the floor;
The province of Munster of the foul clumsy people.
They cannot even twist a sugaun!

SHEAMUS (*coming back*). Here's the hay now.

HANRAHAN. Give it here to me; I'll show ye
what the well-learned, hardy, honest, clever, sensible
Connachtman will do, that has activity and full deft-
ness in his hands, and sense in his head, and courage
in his heart; but that the misfortune and the great
trouble of the world directed him among the *lebidins*
of the province of Munster, without honour, without
nobility, without knowledge of the swan beyond the
duck, or of the gold beyond the brass, or of the lily
beyond the thistle, or of the star of young women, and
the pearl of the white breast, beyond their own share
of sluts and slatterns. Give me a kippeen. (*A man
hands him a stick ; he puts a wisp of hay round it, and
begins twisting it ; and* SHEELA *giving him out the
hay.*)

HANRAHAN.

There is a pearl of a woman giving light to us ;
She is my love ; she is my desire ;
She is fair Oona, the gentle queen-woman.
And the Munstermen do not understand half her
    courtesy.

These Munstermen are blinded by God ;
They do not recognise the swan beyond the grey
    duck ;
But she will come with me, my fine Helen,
Where her person and her beauty shall be praised for
    ever.

Arrah, wisha, wisha, wisha! isn't this the fine village?
isn't this the exceeding village? The village where
there be that many rogues hanged that the people
have no want of ropes with all the ropes that they
steal from the hangman!

> The sensible Connachtman makes
>   A rope for himself ;
> But the Munsterman steals it
>   From the hangman ;
> That I may see a fine rope,
>   A rope of hemp yet,
> A stretching on the throats
>   Of every person here!

On account of one woman only the Greeks departed,
and they never stopped, and they never greatly stayed,
till they destroyed Troy ; and on account of one woman
only this village shall be damned ; *go deo, ma neoir*,
and to the womb of judgment, by God of the graces,
eternally and everlastingly, because they did not
understand that Oona ni Regaun is the second Helen,
who was born in their midst, and that she overcame
in beauty Deirdre and Venus, and all that came before
or that will come after her !

> But she will come with me, my pearl of a woman,
> To the province of Connacht of the fine people ;
> She will receive feasts, wine, and meat,
> High dances, sport, and music !

Oh, wisha, wisha! that the sun may never rise upon
this village ; and that the stars may never shine on

it; and that——. (*He is by this time outside the door. All the men make a rush at the door and shut it.* OONA *runs towards the door, but the women seize her.* SHEAMUS *goes over to her.*)

OONA. Oh! oh! oh! do not put him out; let him back; that is Tumaus Hanrahan—he is a poet—he is a bard—he is a wonderful man. O, let him back; do not do that to him!

SHEAMUS. O Oona *bán, acushla dílis*, let him be; he is gone now, and his share of spells with him! He will be gone out of your head to-morrow; and you will be gone out of his head. Don't you know that I like you better than a hundred thousand Deirdres, and that you are my one pearl of a woman in the world?

HANRAHAN (*outside, beating on the door*). Open, open, open; let me in! Oh, my seven hundred thousand curses on you—the curse of the weak and of the strong—the curse of the poets and of the bards upon you! The curse of the priests on you and the friars! The curse of the bishops upon you, and the Pope! The curse of the widows on you, and the children! Open! (*He beats on the door again and again.*)

SHEAMUS. I am thankful to ye, neighbours; and Oona will be thankful to ye to-morrow. Beat away, you vagabond! Do your dancing out there with yourself now! Isn't it a fine thing for a man to be listening to the storm outside, and himself quiet and easy beside the fire? Beat away, beat away! Where's Connacht now?

THE MARRIAGE

MARTIN, *a young man.*
MARY. *His newly married wife.*
A BLIND FIDDLER.
NEIGHBOURS.

SCENE.—*A cottage kitchen. A table poorly set out, with two cups, a jug of milk, and a cake of bread.* MARTIN *and* MARY *sitting down to it.*

MARTIN. This is a poor wedding dinner I have for you, Mary; and a poor house I brought you to. I wish it was seven thousand times better for your sake.

MARY. Only we have to part again, there wouldn't be in the world a pair happier than myself and yourself; but where's the good of fretting when there's no help for it?

MARTIN. If I had, but a couple of pounds, I could buy a little ass and earn a share of money bringing turf to the big town; or I could job at the fairs. But, my grief, we haven't it, or ten shillings.

MARY. And if I could get but a few hens, and what would feed them, I could be selling the eggs or rearing chickens. But unless God would work a miracle for us, there 's no chance of that itself. (*She wipes her eyes with her apron.*)

MARTIN. Don't be crying, Mary. You belong to me now ; am I not rich so long as you belong to me ? Whatever place I will go to I will know you are thinking of me.

MARY. That is a true word you say, Martin ; I will never be poor so long as I know you to be thinking of me. No riches at all would be so good as that. There 's a line my poor father used to be saying :—

> 'Cattle and gold, store and goods,
>   They pass away like the high floods.'

It was Raftery, the blind man, said that. I never saw him ; but my father used to be talking of him.

MARTIN. I don't care what he said. I wish we had goods and store. He said the exact contrary another time :—

> 'Brogues in the fashion, a good house,
>   Are better than the bare sky over us.'

MARY. Poor Raftery! he 'd give us all that if he had the chance. He was always a good friend to the poor. I heard them saying the other day he was lying in his sickness at some place near Killeenan, and near his death. The Lord have mercy on him !

MARTIN. The Lord have mercy on him, indeed.

Come now, Mary, eat the first bit in your own house.
I 'll take the eggs off the fire.

(*He gets up and goes to the fire.   There is a knock
at the half-door, and an old ragged, patched fiddler puts
in his head.*)

FIDDLER. God save all here !

MARY (*standing up*). Aurah, the poor man, bring
him in.

MARTIN. Let there be sense on you, Mary ; we
have not anything at all to give him.   I will tell him
the way to the Brennans' house : there will be plenty
to find there.

MARY. Indeed and surely I will not put him from
this door.   This is the first time I ever had a house of
my own ; and I will not send anyone at all from my
own door this day.

MARTIN. Do as you think well yourself.   (MARY
goes to the door and opens it.)   Come in, honest
man, and sit down, and a hundred welcomes before
you.   (*The old man comes in, feeling about him as if
blind.*)

MARY. O Martin, he is blind.   May God preserve
him !

OLD MAN. That is so, acushla ; I am in my blindness ; and it is a tired, vexed, blind man I am.   I am
going and ever going since morning, and I never
found a bit to eat since I rose.

MARY. You did not find a bit to eat since morning!
Are you starving ?

OLD MAN. Oh, indeed, there was food to be got if

I would take it; but the bit that does not come from a willing heart, there would be no taste on it; and that is what I did not get since morning; but people putting a potato or a bit of bread out of the door to me, as if I was a dog, with the hope I would not stop, but would go away.

MARY. Oh, sit down with us now, and eat with us. Bring him to the table, Martin. (MARTIN *gives his hand to the old man, and gives him a chair, and puts him sitting at the table with themselves. He makes two halves of the cake, and gives a half to the blind man, and one of the eggs. The old man eats eagerly.*)

OLD MAN. I leave my seven hundred thousand blessings on the people of this house. The blessing of God and Mary on them.

MARY. That it may be well with you. O Martin, that is the first blessing I got in my own house. That blessing is better to me than gold.

OLD MAN. Aurah, is it not beautiful for people to have a house of their own, and to have eyes to look about with?

MARTIN. May God preserve you, right man; it is likely it is a poor thing to be without sight.

OLD MAN. You do not understand, nor any person that has his sight, what it is to be blind and dark the way I am. Not to have before you and behind you but the night. Oh, darkness, darkness! No shape or form in anything; not to see the bird you hear singing in the tree over your head; nor the flower you smell on the bush, or the child, and he laughing in his mother's breast. The morning and the evening, the day and the night, only the same thing to you. Oh, it is a poor thing to be blind! (MARTIN *puts over the other half of the cake and the egg to* MARY, *and makes a sign to her to eat. She makes a sign to him to take a share of them. The blind man stretches his hand over the table to try for a crumb of bread, for he has eaten his own share; and he gets hold of the other half cake and takes it.*)

MARY. Eat that, poor man, it is likely there is hunger on you. Here is another egg for you. (*She puts the other egg in his hand.*)

BLIND MAN. The blessing of the Only Son and of the Holy Mother on the hand that gives it. (MARTIN *puts up his two hands as if dissatisfied; and he is going to say something when* MARY *takes the words from his mouth, laughing at his gloomy face.*)

BLIND MAN. *Maisead,* my blessing on the mouth that laughter came from, and my blessing on the light heart that let it out of the mouth.

MARTIN. A light heart, is it! There is not a light heart with Mary to-night, my grief!

BLIND MAN. Mary is your wife?

MARTIN. She is. I made her my wife three hours ago.

BLIND MAN. Three hours ago?

MARTIN (*bitterly*).—That is so. We were married to-day; and it is at our wedding dinner you are sitting.

BLIND MAN. Your wedding dinner! Do not be mocking me! There is no company here.

MARY. Oh, he is not mocking you ; he would not do a thing like that. There is no company here ; for we have nothing in the house to give them.

BLIND MAN. But you gave it to me ! Is it the truth you are speaking ? Am I the only person that was asked to your wedding ?

MARY. You are. But that is to the honour of God ; and we would never have told you that, but Martin let slip the word from his mouth.

BLIND MAN. Oh, and I eat your little feast on you, and without knowing it.

MARY. It is not without a welcome you eat it.

MARTIN. I am well pleased you came in ; you were more in want of it than ourselves. If we have a bare house now, we might have a full house yet ; and a good dinner on the table to share with those in need of it. I 'd be better off now ; but all the little money I had I laid it out on the house, and the little patch of land. I thought I was wise at the time ; but now we have the house, and we haven't what will keep us alive in it. I have the potatoes set in the garden ; but I haven't so much as a potato to eat. We are left bare, and I am guilty of it.

MARY. If there is any fault, it is on me it is ; coming maybe to be a drag on Martin, where I have no fortune at all. The little money I gained in service, I lost it all on my poor father, when he took sick. And I went back into service ; and the mistress I had was a cross woman ; and when Martin saw the way she was treating me, he wouldn't let me stop with her any more, but he made me his wife. And now I will have great courage, when I have to go out to service again.

BLIND MAN. Will you have to be parted again?

MARTIN. We will, indeed; I must go as a *spailpin fanac*, to reap and to dig the harvest in some other place. But Mary and myself have it settled, we'll meet again at this house on a certain day, with the blessing of God. I'll have the key in my pocket; and we'll come in, with a better chance of stopping in it. You'll have your own cows yet, Mary; and your calves and your firkins of butter, with the help of God.

MARY. I think I hear carts on the road. (*She gets up, and goes to the door.*)

MARTIN. It's the people coming back from the fair. Shut the door, Mary; I wouldn't like them to see how bare the house is; and I'll put a smear of ashes on the window, the way they won't see we're here at all.

BLIND MAN (*raising his head suddenly*). Do not do that; but open the door wide, and let the blessing of God come in on you. (MARY *opens the door again. He takes up his fiddle and begins to play on it. A little boy puts in his head at the door; and then another head is seen, and another with that again.*)

BLIND MAN. Who is that at the door?

MARY. Little boys that came to listen to you.

BLIND MAN. Come in, boys. (*Three or four come inside.*)

BLIND MAN. Boys, I am listening to the carts coming home from the fair. Let you go out, and stop the people; tell them they must come in : there is a wedding-dance here this evening.

BOY. The people are going home. They wouldn't stop for us.

BLIND MAN. Tell them to come in ; and there will be as fine a dance as ever they saw. But they must all give a present to the man and woman that are newly married.

ANOTHER BOY. Why would they come in ? They can have a dance of their own at any time. There is a piper in the big town.

BLIND MAN. Say to them that *I myself* tell them to come in ; and to bring every one a present to the newly-married woman.

BOY. And who are you yourself?

BLIND MAN. Tell them it is Raftery the poet is here, and that is calling to them.

(*The boys run out, tumbling over one another.*)

MARTIN. Are you Raftery, the great poet I heard talk of since I was born ! (*taking his hand*). Seven hundred thousand welcomes before you ; and it is a great honour to us you to be here.

MARY. Raftery the poet ! Now there is luck on us ! The first man that brought us his blessing, and that eat food in my own house, he to be Raftery the poet ! And I hearing the other day you were sick and near your death. And I see no sign of sickness on you now.

BLIND MAN. I am well, I am well now, the Lord be praised for it.

MARTIN. I heard talk of you as often as there are fingers on my hands, and toes on my feet. But indeed I never thought to have the luck of seeing you.

MARY. And it is you that made 'County Mayo,' and the 'Repentance,' and ' The Weaver,' and the ' Shining Flower.' It is often I thought there should be no woman in the world so proud as Mary Hynes, with the way you praised her.

BLIND MAN. O my poor Mary Hynes, without luck ! (*They hear the wheels of a cart outside the house, and an old farmer comes in, a frieze coat on him.*)

OLD FARMER. God save you, Martin ; and is this your wife ? God be with you, woman of the house. And, O Raftery, seven hundred thousand welcomes before you to this country. I would sooner see you than King George. When they told me you were here, I said to myself I would not go past without seeing you, if I didn't get home till morning.

BLIND MAN. But didn't you get my message ?

OLD FARMER. What message is that ?

BLIND MAN. Didn't they tell you to bring a present to the new-married woman and her husband. What have you got for them ?

OLD FARMER. Wait till I see ; I have something in the cart. (*He goes out.*)

MARTIN. O Raftery, you see now what a great name you have here. (*Old farmer comes in again with a bag of meal on his shoulders. He throws it on the floor.*)

OLD FARMER. Four bags of meal I was bringing from the mill ; and there is one of them for the woman of the house.

MARY. A thousand thanks to God and you. (MARTIN *carries the bag to other side of table.*)

BLIND MAN. Now don't forget the fiddler. (*He takes a plate and holds it out.*)

OLD FARMER. I 'll not break my word, Raftery, the first time you came to this country. There is two shillings for you in the plate. (*He throws the money into it.*)

BLIND MAN.

> This is a man has love to God,
> Opening his hand to give out food ;
> Better a small house filled with wheat,
> Than a big house that 's bare of meat.

OLD FARMER. *Maisead,* long life to you, Raftery.

BLIND MAN. Are you there, boy ?

BOY. I am.

BLIND MAN. I hear more wheels coming. Go out, and tell the people Raftery will let no person come in here without a present for the woman of the house.

BOY. I am going. (*He goes out.*)

OLD FARMER. They say there was not the like of you for a poet in Connacht these hundred years back.

(*A middle-aged woman comes in, a pound of tea and a parcel of sugar in her hand.*)

Q

WOMAN. God save all here! I heard Raftery the poet was in it; and I brought this little present to the woman of the house. (*Puts them into* MARY'S *hands*.) I would sooner see Raftery than be out there in the cart.

BLIND MAN. Don't forget the fiddler, O right woman.

WOMAN. And are you Raftery?

BLIND MAN.

> I am Raftery the poet,
>   Full of gentleness and love;
> With eyes without light,
>   With quietness, without misery.

WOMAN. Good the man.

BLIND MAN.

> Quick, quick, quick, for no man
> Need speak twice to a handy woman;
> I 'll praise you when I hear the clatter
> Of your shilling on my platter.

(*A young man comes in with a side of bacon in his arms, and stands waiting.*)

WOMAN. Indeed, I would not begrudge it to you if it was a piece of gold I had (*puts shilling in plate*). The 'Repentance' you made is at the end of my fingers. Here 's another customer for you now. (*The young man comes forward, and gives the bacon to* MARTIN, *who puts it with the meal.*)

MARY. I thank you kindly. Oh, it 's like the miracle worked for Saint Colman, sending him his dinner in the bare hills!

BLIND MAN.

    May that young man with yellow hair
    Find yellow money everywhere!

FAIR YOUNG MAN. I heard the world and his wife were stopping at the door to give a welcome to Raftery, and I thought I would not be behindhand. And here is something for the fiddler (*puts money in the plate*). I would sooner see that fiddler than any other fiddler in the world.

BLIND MAN.

    May that young man with yellow hair
    Buy cheap, sell dear, in every fair.

FAIR YOUNG MAN (*to* MARTIN). How does he know I have yellow hair and he blind? How does he know that?

MARTIN. Hush, my head is going round with the wonder is on me.

MARY. No wonder at all in that. Maybe it is dreaming we all are.

(*A grey-haired man and two girls come in.*)

GREY-HAIRED MAN (*laying down a sack*). The blessing of God here! I heard Raftery was here in the wedding-house, and that he would let no one in without a present. There was nothing in the cart with us but a sack of potatoes, and there it is for you, ma'am.

MARY. Oh, it's too good you all are to me. Whether it's asleep or awake I am, I thank you kindly.

BLIND MAN. Don't forget the fiddler.

GREY-HAIRED MAN. Are you Raftery?

BLIND MAN.

> Who will give Raftery a shilling?
> Here is his platter: who is willing?
> Who will give honour to the poet?
> Here is his platter: show it, show it.

GREY-HAIRED FARMER. You 're welcome; you 're welcome! That is Raftery, anyhow! (*Puts money in the plate.*)

BLIND MAN.

> Come hither girls, give what you can
> To the poor old travelling man.

GREY-HAIRED MAN. Aurah Susan, aurah Oona, are you looking at who is before you, the greatest poet in Ireland? That is Raftery himself. It is often you heard talk of the girl that got a husband with the praises he gave her. If he gives you the same, maybe you 'll get husbands with it.

FIRST GIRL. I often heard talk of Raftery.

THE OTHER GIRL. There was always a great name on Raftery. (*They put some money in the plate shyly.*)

BLIND MAN.

> Before you go, give what you can
> To this young girl and this young man.

FIRST GIRL (*to* MARY). Here 's a couple of dozen of eggs, and welcome.

THE OTHER GIRL. O woman of the house! I have nothing with me here; but I have a good clucking hen at home, and I 'll bring her to you to-morrow; our house is close by.

MARY. Indeed, that's good news to me ; such nice neighbours to be at hand. (*Several men and women come into the house together, every one of them carrying something.*)

SEVERAL (*together*). Welcome, Raftery !

BLIND MAN.

> If ye have hearts are worth a mouse,
> Welcome the bride into her house.

(*They laugh and greet* MARY, *and put down gifts—a roll of butter, rolls of woollen thread, and many other things.*)

OLD FARMER. Ha, ha! That's right. They are coming in now. Now, Raftery ; isn't it generous and open-handed and liberal this country is ? Isn't it better than the County Mayo ?

BLIND MAN.

> I'd say all Galway was rich land,
> If I'd your shillings in my hand.

(*Holds out his plate to them.*)

OLD FARMER (*laughing*). Now, neighbours, down with it ! My conscience ! Raftery knows how to get hold of the money.

A MAN OF THEM. *Maisead*, he doesn't own much riches ; and there is pride on us all to see him in this country. (*Puts money in the plate, and all the others do the same. A lean old man comes in.*)

MARTIN (*to* MARY). That is John the Miser, or Seagan na Stucaire, as they call him. That is the man that is hardest in this country. He never gave a penny to any person since he was born.

MISER. God save all here! Oh, is that Raftery?
Ho, ho! God save you Raftery, and a hundred
thousand welcomes before you to this country.
There is pride on us all to see you. There is gladness on the whole country, you to be here in our
midst. If you will believe me, neighbours, I saw
with my own eyes the bush Raftery put his curse on ;
and as sure as I'm living, it was withered away.
There is nothing of it but a couple of old twigs now.

BLIND MAN.

> I've heard a voice like his before,
> And liked some little voice the more ;
> I'd sooner have, if I'd my choice,
> A big heart and a small voice.

MISER. Ho! ho! Raftery, making poems as usual.
Well, there is great joy on us, indeed, to see you
in our midst.

BLIND MAN. What is the present you have
brought to the new-married woman ?

MISER. What is the present I brought? O
maisead! the times are too bad on a poor man. I
brought a few fleeces of wool I had to the market to-
day, and I couldn't sell it ; I had to bring it home
again. And calves I had there, I couldn't get any
buyer for at all. There is misfortune on these times.

BLIND MAN. Every person that came in brought
his own present with him. There is the new-married
woman, and let you put down a good present.

MISER. O *maisead*, much good may it do her! (*He
takes out of his pocket a small parcel of snuff ; takes a*

*piece of paper from the floor, and pours into it, slowly
and carefully, a little of the snuff, and puts it on the
table.*)

BLIND MAN.

> Look at the gifts of every kind
> Were given with a willing mind ;
> After all this, it 's not enough
> From the man of cows—a pinch of snuff!

OLD FARMER. *Maisead,* long life to you, Raftery ;
that your tongue may never lose its edge.   That is a
man of cows certainly ; I myself am a man of sheep.

BLIND MAN. A bag of meal from the man of
sheep.

FAIR YOUNG MAN. And I am a man of pigs.

BLIND MAN. A side of meat from the man of
pigs.

MARTIN. Don't forget the woman of hens.

BLIND MAN.

> A pound of tea from the woman of hens.
> After all this, it 's not enough
> From the man of cows—a pinch of snuff!

ALL. After all this, it 's not enough

> From the man of cows—a pinch of snuff!

OLD FARMER. The devil the like of such fun have
we had this year !

MISER. Oh, indeed, I was only keeping a little
grain for myself ; but it 's likely they may want it all.
(*He takes the paper out, and lays it on the table.*)

BLIND MAN. A bag of meal from the man of
sheep.

ALL. After all this, it's not enough

From the man of cows—a half-ounce of snuff !

(*One of the girls hands the snuff round ; they laugh and sneeze, taking pinches of it.*)

OLD FARMER. My soul to the devil, Seagan, do the thing decently. Give out one of those fleeces you have in the cart with you.

MISER. I never saw the like of you for fools since I was born. Is it mad you are ?

ALL. From the man of cows, a half-ounce of snuff !

MISER. Oh, *maisead*, if there must be a present put down, take the fleece, and my share of misfortune on you ! (*Three or four of the boys run out.*)

OLD FARMER. Aurah, Seagan, what is your opinion of Raftery now ? He has you destroyed worse than the bush ! (*The boys come back, a fleece with them.*)

BOY. Here is the fleece, and it's very heavy it is. (*They put it down, and there falls a little bag out of it that bursts and scatters the money here and there on the floor.*)

MISER. Ub-ub-bu ! That is my share of money scattered on me that I got for my calves. (*He stoops down to gather it together. All the people burst out laughing again.*)

OLD FARMER. *Maisead*, Seagan, where did you get the money ? You told us you didn't sell your share of calves.

BLIND MAN.

> He that got good gold
> For calves he never sold
> Must put good money down
> With a laugh, without a frown ;
> Or I 'll destroy that man
> With a bone-breaking rann.
> I'll rhyme him by the book
> To a blue-watery look.

MISER. Oh, Raftery, don't do that. I tasted enough of your ranns just now, and I don't want another taste of them. There 's threepence for you. (*He puts three pennies in the plate.*)

BLIND MAN.

> I 'll put a new name upon
> This strong farmer, of Thrippeny John.
> He 'll be called, without a doubt,
> Thrippeny John from this time out.
> Put your sovereign on my plate,
> Or that and worse will be your fate.

MISER. O, in the name of God, Raftery, stop your mouth and let me go ! Here is the sovereign for you ; and indeed it 's not with my blessing I give it.

(BLIND MAN *plays on the fiddle. They all stand up and dance but* SEAGAN NA STUCAIRE, *who shakes his fist in* BLIND MAN'S *face, and goes out.*

When they have danced for a minute or two, BLIND MAN *stops fiddling and stands up.*)

BLIND MAN. I was near forgetting : I am the only person here gave nothing to the woman of the house.

(*Hands the plate of money to* MARY.) Take that and my seven hundred blessings along with it, and that you may be as well as I wish you to the end of life and time. Count the money now, and see what the neighbours did for you.

MARY. That is too much indeed.

MARTIN. You have too much done for us already.

BLIND MAN. Count it, count it; while I go over and try can I hear what sort of blessings Seagan na Stucaire is leaving after him.

(*Neighbours all crowd round counting the money.* BLIND MAN *goes to the door, looks back with a sigh, and goes quietly out.*)

OLD FARMER. Well, you have enough to set you up altogether, Martin. You 'll be buying us all up within the next six months.

MARTIN. Indeed I don't think I 'll be going digging potatoes for other men this year, but to be working for myself at home.

(*The sound of horse's steps are heard. A young man comes into the house.*)

YOUNG MAN. What is going on here at all? All the cars in the country gathered at the door, and Seagan na Stucaire going swearing down the road.

OLD FARMER. Oh, this is the great wedding was made by Raftery.—Where is Raftery? Where is he gone?

MARTIN (*going to the door*). He 's not here. I don't see him on the road. (*Turns to young farmer.*)

Did you meet a blind fiddler going out the door—
the poet Raftery?

YOUNG MAN. The poet Raftery? I did not; but
I stood by his grave at Killeenan three days ago.

MARY. His grave? Oh, Martin, it was a dead man
was in it!

MARTIN. Whoever it was, it was a man sent by
God was in it.

THE LOST SAINT

An Old Man.
A Teacher.
Conall and other Children.

Scene.—*A large room as it was in the old time. A long table in it. A troop of children, a share of them eating their dinner, another share of them sitting after eating. There is a teacher stooping over a book in the other part of the room.*

A Child (*standing up*). Come out, Felim, till we see the new hound.

Another Child. We can't. The master told us not to go out till we would learn this poem, the poem he was teaching us to-day.

Another Child. He won't let anyone at all go out till he can say it.

Another Child. *Maisead*, disgust for ever on the same old poem ; but there is no fear for myself—I'll get out, never fear; I'll remember it well enough. But I don't think you will get out, Conall. Oh, there is the master ready to begin.

TEACHER (*lifting up his head*). Now, children, have you finished your dinner?

CHILDREN. Not yet. (*A poor-looking, grey old man comes to the door.*)

A CHILD. Oh, that is old Cormacin that grinds the meal for us, and minds the oven.

OLD MAN. The blessing of God here! Master, will you give me leave to gather up the scraps, and to bring them out with me?

MASTER. You may do that. (*To the children.*) Come here now, till I see if you have that poem right, and I will let you go out when you have it said.

FEARALL. We are coming; but wait a minute till I ask old Cormacin what is he going to do with the leavings he has there.

OLD MAN. I am gathering them to give to the birds, avourneen.

TEACHER. We will do it now; come over here. (*The children stand together in a row.*)

TEACHER. Now I will tell you who made the poem you are going to say to me: There was a holy, saintly man in Ireland some years ago. Aongus Ceile Dé was the name he had. There was no man in Ireland had greater humility than he. He did not like the people to be giving honour to him, or to be saying he was a great saint, or that he made fine poems. It was because of his humility he stole away one night, and put a disguise on himself; and he went like a poor man through the country, working for his own living without anyone knowing him. He is gone away out of knowledge now, without anyone at all knowing where he is. Maybe he is feeding pigs or grinding meal now like any other poor person.

A CHILD. Grinding meal like old Cormacin here.

TEACHER. Exactly. But before he went away, it is many fine sweet poems he made in the praise of God and the angels ; and it was one of those I was teaching you to-day.

A CHILD. What is the name you said he had?

TEACHER. Aongus Ceile Dé, the servant of God. They gave him that name because he was so holy. Now, Felim, say the first two lines you ; and Art will say the two next lines; and Aodh the two lines after that, and so on to the end.

FELIM.

> Up in the kingdom of God, there are
> Archangels for every single day.

ART.

> And it is they certainly
> That steer the entire week.

AODH.

> The first day is holy ;
> Sunday belongs to God.

FERGUS.

> Gabriel watches constantly
> Every week over Monday.

CONALL.

> Gabriel watches constantly—

TEACHER. That's not it, Conall; Fergus said that.

CONALL. It is to God Sunday belongs——

TEACHER. That's not it; that was said before. It is at Tuesday we are now. Who is it has Tuesday? (*The little boy does not answer.*) Who is it has Tuesday? Don't be a fool, now.

CONALL (*putting the joint of his finger in his eye*). I don't know.

TEACHER. Oh, my shame you are! Look now; go in the place Fearall is, and he will go in your place. Now, Fearall.

FEARALL.

> It is true that Tuesday is kept
> By Michael in his full strength.

TEACHER. That's it. Now, Conall, say who has Monday.

CONALL. I can't.

TEACHER. Say the two lines before that and I will be satisfied. Who has Monday?

CONALL (*crying*). I don't know.

TEACHER. Oh, aren't you the little amadan! I will never put anything at all in your head. I will not let you go out till you know that poem. Now, boys, run out with you; and we will leave Conall Amadan here. (*The* TEACHER *and all the other scholars go out.*)

THE OLD MAN. Don't be crying, avourneen; I will teach the poem to you; I know it myself.

CONALL. Aurah, Cormacin, I cannot learn it. I am not clever or quick like the other boys. I can't put anything in my head (*bursts into crying again*). I have no memory for anything.

OLD MAN (*laying his hand on his head*). Take courage, astore. You will be a wise man yet, with the help of God. Come with me now, and help me to divide these scraps. (*The child gets up.*) That's it now; dry your eyes and don't be discouraged.

CONALL (*wiping his eyes*). What are you making three shares of the scraps for?

THE OLD MAN. I am going to give the first share to the geese; I am putting all the cabbage on this dish for them; and when I go out, I will put a grain of meal on it, and it will feed them finely. I have scraps of meat here, and old broken bread, and I will give that to the hens; they will lay their eggs better when they will get food like that. These little crumbs are for the little birds that do be singing to me in the morning, and that awaken me with their share of music. I have oaten meal for them. (*Sweeps the floor, and gathers little crumbs of bread.*) I have a great wish for the little birds. (*The old man looks up; he sees the little boy lying on a cushion, and he asleep. He stands a little while looking at him. Tears gather in his eyes; then he goes down on his knees.*)

OLD MAN. O Lord, O God, take pity on this little soft child. Put wisdom in his head, cleanse his heart, scatter the mist from his mind, and let him learn his lesson like the other boys. O Lord, Thou wert Thyself young one time : take pity on youth. O Lord, Thou Thyself shed tears : dry the tears of this little lad.

Listen, O Lord, to the prayer of Thy servant, and do not keep from him this little thing he is asking of Thee. O Lord, bitter are the tears of a child, sweeten them ; deep are the thoughts of a child, quiet them ; sharp is the grief of a child, take it from him ; soft is the heart of a child, do not harden it.

(*While the old man is praying, the* TEACHER *comes in. He makes a sign to the children outside ; they come in and gather about him. The old man notices the children ; he starts up, and shame burns on him.*)

TEACHER. I heard your prayer, old man ; but there is no good in it. I praise you greatly for it, but that child is half-witted. I prayed to God myself once or twice on his account, but there was no good in it.

THE OLD MAN. Perhaps God heard me. God is for the most part ready to hear. The time we ourselves are empty without anything, God listens to us; and He does not think on the thing we are without, but gives us our fill.

TEACHER. It is the truth you are speaking; but there is no good in praying this time. This boy is very ignorant. (*He and the old man go over to the child, who is still asleep, and signs of tears on his cheeks.*) He must work hard, and very hard ; and maybe with the dint of work, he will get a little learning some time. (*He puts his hand on the cheek of the little boy, and he starts up, and wonder on him when he sees them all about him.*)

THE OLD MAN. Ask it to him now.

TEACHER. Do you remember the poem now, Conall?

R

CONALL.

> Up in the heaven of God, there are
> Archangels for every day.
>
> And it is they certainly
> That steer the entire week.
>
> The first day is holy ;
> Sunday belongs to God.
>
> Gabriel watches constantly
> Every week over Monday.
>
> It is true that Tuesday is kept
> By Michael in his full strength.
>
> Rafael, honest and kind and gentle,
> It is to him Wednesday belongs.
>
> To Sachiel, that is without crookedness,
> Thursday belongs every week.
>
> Haniel, the Archangel of God,
> It is he has Friday.
>
> Bright Cassiel, of the blue eyes,
> It is he directs Saturday.

TEACHER. That is a great wonder, not a word failed on him. But tell me, Conall astore, how did you learn that poem since?

CONALL. When I was sleeping, just now, there came an old man to me, and I thought there was every colour that is in the rainbow upon him. And he took hold of my shirt, and he tore it; and then he opened my breast, and he put the poem within in my heart.

OLD MAN. It is God that sent that dream to you. I have no doubt you will not be hard to teach from this out.

CONALL. And the man that came to me, I thought it was old Cormacin that was in it.

FEARALL. Maybe it was Aongus Ceile Dé himself that was in it.

AODH. Maybe Cormacin is Aongus.

TEACHER. Are you Aongus Ceile Dé? I desire you in the name of God to tell me.

THE OLD MAN (*bowing his head*). Oh, you have found it out now! Oh, I thought no one at all would ever know me. My grief that you have found me out!

TEACHER (*going on his knees*). O holy Aongus, forgive me; give me your blessing. O holy man, give your blessing to these children. (*The children fall on their knees round him.*)

THE OLD MAN (*stretching out his hand*). The blessing of God on you. The blessing of Christ and His Holy Mother on you. My own blessing on you.

THE NATIVITY

Two Women.   Kings.
Shepherds.   Child Angels.
The Holy Family.

SCENE.—*A stable. The door shut on it. The dawn of day is rising, and the colours of morning coming. Two women come in—a woman of them from the east, and a woman from the west, and they tired from the journey. There is a branch of a cherry tree in the hand of one of them, and a flock of flax in the hand of the other of them.*

THE FIRST WOMAN. God be with you!
THE SECOND WOMAN. God be with yourself!
FIRST WOMAN. Where are you going?
SECOND WOMAN. In search of a woman I am.
FIRST WOMAN. And myself as well as you.
SECOND WOMAN. That is strange. What woman is that?
FIRST WOMAN. A woman that is about to give birth to a child; and I think it would be well for her, another woman to be giving care to her.

SECOND WOMAN. That is the same woman I am in search of in the same way.

FIRST WOMAN. I did an unkindness to her, and grief and shame came on me after, and I thought to make up for it if I could.

FIRST WOMAN. Oh, that is just the same thing I myself did.

SECOND WOMAN. That is a wonder. I will tell you how it happened with me; and you will tell me your story after that.

FIRST WOMAN. I will tell it.

SECOND WOMAN. That is good. I was one evening a while ago getting ready the supper for my husband and my children, when there came a man and a young woman to the door, and the woman riding an ass. They asked a night's lodging of me. They said it was up to Jerusalem they were going. But, my grief! the husband I have is a rough man, and there was fear on me to let them in; I was afraid he would do something to me, and I refused them. They said to me they were very tired; and they pressed so hard on me that I told them at last to go out and sleep in the barn, in the place the flax was, and my husband would not have knowledge of it. But about midnight my husband was struck with sickness, and a great pain came on him of a sudden, as if his death was near. When I thought him to be dying, I was in dread; and I ran out to the people I had put in the barn, asking help from them.

THE FIRST WOMAN. God help us!

SECOND WOMAN. God help us, indeed! And when
the woman that was lying on the stalks of flax heard
my story, it is what she did : she took a flock of the
husks of the flax that were on the floor, and said to
me: ‘Lay that,’ she said, ‘ on the place the pain is, and
it will cure him.’   Out with me as quick as I could,
and the husks in my hand, the same as they are now.
My husband was on the point of death at that time ;
but, as sure as I am alive, when I put the husks on
him, the pain went away, and he was as well as ever
he was.

FIRST WOMAN. That is a great story!

SECOND WOMAN. And when I ran out again to
bring the woman in with me, she was gone ; and
I heard a voice, as I thought, saying these two
lines :—

> ‘ A meek woman and a rough man ;
> The Son of God lying in husks.’

FIRST WOMAN. You heard that said ?

SECOND WOMAN. There was grief and shame on
me then, letting her from me like that, without giving
her thanks, or anything at all ; and I followed her on
the morrow, for I said to myself that she was blessed.
I heard she was gone to Bethlehem ; and I followed
her to this stable ; for I thought I could be helpful
to her, and she in that state.   They told me she was
not in the inn ; and that there was no place at all for
her to get, till she came to this stable.

FIRST WOMAN. Is not that wonderful ? You said

the truth when you said it was a blessed woman that was in it.

SECOND WOMAN. How do you know that?

FIRST WOMAN. Because she did a great marvel under my own eyes. My sorrow and my bitter grief! I did a thing seven times worse than what you did. It was fear before your husband was on you when you refused her the night's lodging; but the hardness and the misery in my own heart made me refuse her fruit she asked of me. She herself and the man that was with her were going by; and the day came close on her and hot, and there was a large tree of cherries in my garden. She looked up then, and she took a longing for them. 'O right woman!' she said; 'there is a desire come on me to have a few of your cherries; maybe you will give me a share of them.' 'I will not give them,' said I, 'to any stranger at all travelling the road like yourself.' 'Give them to me, if it is your will,' says she, quiet, and nice, and gentle, 'for I am not far from the birth of my child; and I have a great longing for them.'

I don't know what was the bad thing was in my heart; but I refused her again. No sooner was the word out of my mouth than the big tree bent down of itself to her, and laid its twigs across the wall, and out on the road, till she could put out her hand and take her fill of the cherries.

SECOND WOMAN. That was a great miracle, without doubt.

FIRST WOMAN. It was so; and grief came to me

after that for refusing her ; for I knew by it that God had a hand in her. And I took this branch in my hand, and I followed her to the stable to ask pardon of her.

SECOND WOMAN. Is it not a wonder how we came here together on the same search?

FIRST WOMAN. I think she will be wanting help, for they said to me in the inn she was not far from the birth of her child ; and I made as good haste as I could. Maybe we are in time to give her help yet.

SECOND WOMAN. I will knock at the door.

FIRST WOMAN. Do so.

SECOND WOMAN. Wait a while ; there are strangers coming up this road from the west.

FIRST WOMAN. That is so ; and look on the other side : there are great people coming from the east. We must wait till they go past. (*They sit down on either side of the door. Kings, finely dressed, come in at the east side ; and herds and shepherds on the west side.*)

A KING (*pointing upwards with his hand*). Kings and friends, it is not possible I am mistaken. Is not the wonderful star we followed as far as this standing now without stirring over this place?

A SHEPHERD. O friends, look up. There is not a bird in the sky that is not gathered above this house.

A KING. We are come from the east, from the rising of the sun, a long, long way off from this country, following the star that is standing still over us now. Where are you come from, shepherds?

A SHEPHERD. We are come from the west, from the setting of the sun, a long way off from this country.

KING. And what is it brought you here? I dare say it is not without cause yourselves and ourselves are met at the door of this house.

SHEPHERD. We were sitting one evening quiet and satisfied on a grassy hill watching our flocks; and we saw all of a sudden a thing that put wonder on us. The lambs that were sucking at the ewes left off sucking, and they looked up in the sky; and the kids that were drinking at the pool stopped drinking and looked up. It would put wonder on any person at all to see the little kids looking up as wise as ourselves. We looked up then, and we saw a beautiful bright angel over our heads; and fear came on us; but the angel spoke, and he said to us that some great joy was coming into the world, and he said: ' Set out now in search of it, and go to Bethlehem.' ' Where is that?' we asked. ' In a country that is called Judea,' said the angel, ' a long, long way from you to the east.' We made ourselves ready on the morrow; and there was every sort of bird that was in the sky going before us. Look at them all now, a share of them sitting on the roof of the house, and thousands of others above in a great cloud. We are all simple people, poor shepherds, it is not fitting for us to be coming here; but there was fear on us when we heard the angel speak.

KING. It is great powerful kings we are. We come from far off, from the rising of the sun. There is not a king or a prince in these parts is fit to be put beside the lowest steward we have. And we are wise. There is no knowledge or learning to be had under the sun that we have not got. But now we are brought by the guidance of that star to the Master and the Teacher that will teach us all the knowledge and wisdom of the whole world. It is in that hope we are come following this star. And now, shepherds, tell us what is it you want here.

SHEPHERD. We cannot say rightly what we want here. But the angel told us there was some great joy coming into the world; and we followed the birds in search of that joy, and the birds came to this place.

KING. It is likely, since the star of knowledge led us, and the birds led you, to the one place, that there is some wonderful thing in it. O friends, whatever thing is in this closed stable, it is certain it will put great fear or great joy, or maybe great sorrow, on these shepherds and on ourselves.

SHEPHERD. You who are noble and great, and rich and wise, and learned in all things, tell us what is in this stable.

KING. It is true we are noble and honourable, and learned and powerful, and wise and prudent, but we cannot tell you that. We do not know ourselves what is the thing that is in it.

SHEPHERD. Tell us this much anyway, is it sorrow or joy, grief or gladness, courage or fear, it will put on us ? Will you not tell us that before we knock at the closed door ?

KING. It is certain there are no other persons in the world so learned as ourselves. We are astronomers to tell of the coming and going of the stars, and the ways of the heavens, and everything that is on the earth and in the clouds and under the earth. But for all that we cannot tell you this thing.

SHEPHERD. Who will knock at the door ?

KING. It is my advice to you now : the king that is youngest of us, and the shepherd that is youngest of you, to go to the door and to knock together.

SHEPHERD. Why do you say the youngest king and the youngest shepherd ?

KING. Do you not know there is no person free from sin but only infants that have never found occasion of doing it ? The man that is youngest of us, it is he found least occasion to do wrong ; and he is the best fitted to knock at this door, whatever there may be inside it.

SHEPHERD (*leading out another shepherd*). This is the man that is youngest among us.

KING (*leading out another king*). This is the youngest king in our company.

(*The two go to the door together and knock at it. The door is opened by St. Joseph, and the manger is seen, and Mary Mother kneeling beside the manger on her two knees, her hands crossed on her breast, and she praying.*)

KING. We are come to this door to do honour to God, and to Him that God has sent. It is here all the people of the whole world will be taught, and will be put on the road that is best. Show Him to us; and we will proclaim Him to all the people of knowledge, and the learned people of the world.

SHEPHERD. We are come in search of Him who is come to put joy in the world, and to put gladness in the hearts of the people. Show Him to us; and we will give news of Him to the herds and the shepherds, and the simple people of the whole world.

ST. JOSEPH. It is great my gladness is to see you here. A hundred welcomes before you, both gentle and simple. Come in, and I will show you Him you are in search of. Look at this baby in the manger. It is He is King of the World, and He will put all the countries of the world under His feet.

MARY MOTHER. He is the Son of God.

(*They all go on their knees.*)

KING. We have brought gifts and offerings with us. Let us show them to you.

MARY MOTHER. Walk softly and quietly, that you may not awake the Child.

A KING. I am the king is oldest in our company. I will walk softly, and I will not awake the Child.

A SHEPHERD. I am the man is oldest among us; let us give our poor gifts to you like the others. I will walk softly; I will not awake the little One.

KING. We have brought from the rising of the sun, gold, and frankincense, and myrrh, and a share of every noble precious treasure there is in the world. It is not possible for the whole world to give a thing we have not with us; and we have brought another thing the world has not to give, the knowledge and sense and wisdom of our own hearts. We have been gathering it through the years, from youth to old age; and we put it first of all these things. (*They lay gold and spices, and other treasures before the Child.*)

SHEPHERD. We have brought fleeces, and cheeses, and a little lamb with us as an offering. We have no other thing to give. We are old now, and we have got this wisdom from God, that there is nothing better worth giving than the things God has given to us. (*They put down their own offerings. The two women come round to the front.*)

THE FIRST WOMAN. Oh, do you see that?

SECOND WOMAN. King of the World, he said! Oh, are we not the unhappy sinners?

FIRST WOMAN. My bitter grief for myself and yourself!

SECOND WOMAN. I am lost for ever. There is no forgiveness for me to find for the thing I did!

FIRST WOMAN. Nor for myself.

SECOND WOMAN. You were not so guilty as I was.

FIRST WOMAN. Let us go; and let us hide ourselves under some scalp of a rock, in a hole in the earth, or in the middle of the woods!

SECOND WOMAN. Let us then hasten that we may hide ourselves.

MARY MOTHER (*rises up and stretches out her hands, beckoning to the women*). Come over here.

Come to this cradle. The Son of God is in this cradle, and His cradle is nothing but a manger. But yet He is King of the World. There is a welcome before the whole world coming to this cradle; but it is those that are asking forgiveness will get the greatest welcome.

(*The two women fall on their knees.*

Child angels come and stand on the rising ground at each side of the stable, and shining clothes on them like the colours of the morning. They lift their trumpets and blow them softly.)

MARY MOTHER. Listen to the angels, the angels of God!

AN ANGEL OF THEM. A hundred welcomes before the whole world to this cradle. We give out peace; we give out goodwill; we give out joy to the whole world! (*They take their share of trumpets up again, and blow them long and very sweetly.*)

THE END.

PRINTED BY PONSONBY & GIBBS at the University Press, Dublin.

For EU product safety concerns, contact us at Calle de José Abascal, 56–1°,
28003 Madrid, Spain or eugpsr@cambridge.org.